STAYING
TOGETHER

STAYING TOGETHER

A practical way to make your relationship
succeed and grow

Reginald Beech

JOHN WILEY & SONS
Chichester · New York · Brisbane · Toronto · Singapore

Copyright © 1985 by John Wiley & Sons Ltd
Text copyright © by John Wiley & Sons Ltd
Cartoon copyright © by Reginald Beech
Reprinted with corrections February 1986

Library of Congress Cataloging in Publication Data:

Beech, H.R.
  Staying together.

  Includes index.
  1. Marriage.   2. Interpersonal conflict.
3. Domestic Relations.   I. Title.
HQ734.B495   1985   646.7′8   85–9567
ISBN 0 471 90809 6

British Library Cataloguing in Publication Data

Beech, H.R.
  Staying together : a practical way to make
your relationship succeed and grow.
  1. Marriage   2. Interpersonal relations
  I. Title
  306.8′72   HQ728

  ISBN 0 471 90809 6

Printed and bound in Great Britain by
Biddles Ltd, Guildford and King's Lynn

To
LOUKIE
GUY
JAMES
DANIEL
and
JONATHAN

CONTENTS

Preface

This book is written for most people, for most of us will marry and most of us are going to have problems with our relationship. Whether you are about to embark upon your special relationship, or ready to end it, this book will offer something. But it is also intended for the many who simply feel that their relationship could stand improvement, and for those attempting reconciliation.

Every day our newspapers inform us of marital problems. 'Millionaire's fourth wife says position made intolerable by husband's new romance,' proclaims one headline, while another tells the terrifying story of a man's strangulation of his three daughters because of his wife's infidelity. Ladies trying to arrange that their divorces are heard in Switzerland (where settlements are better) jostle for a place in the gossip columns with those locking themselves into an ex-husband's mansion to stake a claim to the family fortune.

Sometimes amazing, often amusing, but most frequently tragic, the stories of bitterness, hatred, and enormous hardship arising from broken relationships, catch our attention over breakfast. What is not told – and what can probably never be told – is the quite extraordinary anguish that such problems can cause to the many people involved, including the children of those shattered families. Arguably, the problem is the greatest single threat to our personal happiness as well as a major attack on the v fabric of our society, far outweighing in scale physical illness or automobile accidents. Yet little or nothing seems to be done at a national level to stem the tide, and there are no earnest debates in Parliament or Senate to comment on an intolerable situation. One can be forgiven for thinking that governmental action has focussed entirely on making divorce easier, although the Booth Committee (UK) recently recognized that the child of a broken marriage underachieves at school, is financially penalized, and suffers more physical and psychological health problems. Marriage Guidance Councils have taken some initiatives, and individual clergy are kept busy with these problems, but the growth of marital counseling is outstripped by the increase in marriage failure, and many leading churchmen seem to be more preoccupied with political issues than with individual human tragedy.

Some may object that the word 'love' is rarely mentioned in this book, and others that no firm moral standpoint is offered. Instead, the following pages are solely concerned with the description of strategies aimed at improving relationships. This may seem a little cold or calculating, but it is an approach totally opposed to the lobbies of the disenchanted and embittered that press for individualism, separate development, and the illusory freedom of casual relationships. The view taken here is that staying together makes sense – and is an attainable goal – for most of us.

If I wish, I can raise my eyes to the stars. If I want, I can put on my coat and walk in the rain. If I like, I can switch on the radio or, if I care to do so, I can visit my friend for a chat. We regard the springs of human nature in this way – as activities determined by wishes and desires. We tend to think that all action has to start with a wish to do this or that – and much of what happens *can* be accounted for in this way. But much of human behavior is not easily explained by the 'I wish' or 'I want' interpretation. Few of us would learn our French verbs, or walk through a cold night to visit a sick friend, if this behavior first had to be desirable. The wish and want part has somehow got on to a higher and more complicated level, although we can still argue that we must *want* to do the thing or it wouldn't happen at all. When people face a crisis in their relationship the clear nature of wanting is confused; in fact, the individuals concerned may simultaneously wish for different and quite opposite things, wanting to quit but wanting to stay, and getting frozen in this conflict. Solving the conflict may not depend directly on the strengthening of either a wish to stay or a wish to go, but also on factors that are only indirectly concerned with our immediate desires. Troubled marriages involve people who feel wronged, slighted, neglected, betrayed, and let down by their partners; their immediate wishes and wants are for revenge, punishment of the guilty one, restitution and abject apology from the 'offender.' They seldom see that they, too, may be at fault, that staying together in a mutually rewarding relationship is a joint responsibility. Nor do they seem aware that they could perhaps *do* something about what is happening; constructive ideas are lacking and positive moves seem to be unthinkable.

Yet this is precisely what is needed. Difficult as it may be to accept at first, taking positive and constructive action actually changes the situation, so that the couple can come to modify their attitudes and feelings toward each other. Behavioral approaches take the view that when we change *what we do* we can bring about changes in *how we feel*. For those locked in conflict it isn't easy to accept that this can happen, nor is it simple for them to take even the first faltering steps that are needed. But, as we can't make people *feel* and *want* to be nice to each other, we have no choice but (putting it at its most basic) to have people *behave nice* in order to feel nice. There is plenty of evidence that putting things this way around actually works, however unlikely this may seem at first.

Approaches to marriage failure by counselors and therapists typically do not make use of this basic idea; they often prefer to change the way people think rather than how they behave. More important, most approaches fail to tell people just what it is they should do, leaving them with a willingness to try to sort out their problems but with no clear-cut notion of how to do so. Creating a climate of understanding between the couple may be useful but most of us need to gain a better idea of what we are doing wrong and what we must do to put things right.

In short, there is a need for a set of rules of the kind you might have when starting your vegetable garden – not a book that takes you through an appreciation of the joys of nature, nor one that describes the exotic plants you could consider growing, but a simple guide to which way up to stick the potato in the trench you have just dug. It is not so much that we need to philosophize about conflict, disagreement and breakdown but, rather, an urgent need to know the practical steps we have to take to make relationships work.

Understandably, each partner will be inclined to think that there is only one viewpoint and only one way to put things right – *their* way. After all, the whole problem has been caused by the other person. They may also go on to point out how difficult it is to take steps of the kind described in this book because they are not certain they want the relationship to survive. So far as the first point is concerned, who-was-guilty-of-what is no longer a useful question to ask; settling that point would achieve nothing. What is needed is a commitment *now* to dealing with what will happen in the future and a method for dealing with difficulties that arise. So far as the second point is concerned, it is true that where there is no willingness to try again then failure is inevitable. Either partner, at any time, can easily make reconciliation impossible.

It is vital to realize that, in following the rules for Staying Together, couples are not being asked to sacrifice their self-interest but to actually ensure that their own interests are being taken care of. While the approach described here is not a guarantee of success, it does offer the means by which this can be achieved and a real hope that a new beginning is possible.

Not everything in the program described is needed by every couple. Some will have to follow the rules for dealing with all problem areas in order to get things right, while others may only need a little help and guidance to secure the kind of changes and improvements they are looking for. In fact it is perfectly reasonable to dip into the program and just make use of those parts that are relevant to your own problems, but a look through the whole book will help you decide just what it is that you need and also give you a better understanding of what the whole approach is about.

Certainly, reading the entire book will give you insight into the ways in which we all get things wrong from time to time, as well as counteracting any idea that we come into this world fully equipped with all the skills needed to deal with our relationship problems.

It hardly needs to be said that, while all the examples given are taken directly from actual client material, the details have been changed and modified to conceal the identity of those involved. Everyone reading the book, however, will see in these examples some reflection of their own difficulties and failings since we all fail, at times, to face up to our relationship problems in an effective way.

Finally, it may be that some readers will find the cartoon illustrations by Keef out of place in a book about so serious a subject. In the author's view almost the opposite might be argued, in that a little humor could provide some much-needed light relief. It could also be said that a cartoon can sometimes make the point in a way that is more memorable and with greater impact than the written message.

CHAPTER 1

Marriage Problems: Causes and Cures

Mrs Friday, in her mid-forties, had an affair. It was the first and only time she had departed from a rather strict personal moral code, and she couldn't really explain to anyone why it had happened. It was quite a brief affair, lasting only a couple of weeks and with a man she hardly knew. Certainly, as she told me, she hadn't really liked him very much, and was very relieved when it was all over.

The problem was that, being always a straightforward and conscientious person, her feelings of guilt bothered her and, finally, some few weeks after the affair was over, she felt she simply must confess to her husband. He was overwhelmed by the news, and so profoundly shocked that for some time he couldn't quite grasp the significance of what had happened. However, Mr Friday's behavior underwent an important change: from being a kind and considerate husband, he became sullen, aggressive, and bitter.

Only a few weeks after the matter had first surfaced he told his wife that he simply couldn't go on living with her, that he felt betrayed and could not come to terms with her disloyalty. At that stage he ordered her to leave and, feeling utterly humiliated, completely responsible and, unable to explain even to herself why she had behaved as she had, she prepared to quit the family home. At the last moment before her departure, Mr Friday relented. Although he still felt angry and betrayed, he told her that he would forgive her and try to forget the matter. Mrs Friday was overjoyed at this, and settled down to being an even more considerate and loving wife to her husband.

However, it was not long before Mr Friday's tortured mind turned, once more, to his wife's affair, and he began regular and frequent interrogations of her about it. These took the form of inquiring into the smallest detail of what had happened and what Mrs Friday's feelings had been at the time. Nothing was too unimportant: the number of the house Mrs Friday and her lover had gone to, the state of the wallpaper in the bedroom, the frequency and type of sexual contact and, in short, the minutest detail of the relationship had to be examined in the interrogation sessions.

Mrs Friday eagerly complied with the requests for information, since she thought that, in this way, she could put her husband's mind at rest. Indeed, on his insistence, she racked her brain for more detail to give him, and so make a clean breast of everything that had happened.

As is so often the case, such morbid fascination did not help Mr Friday to come to terms with the problem but, instead, seemed to have the opposite effect. In fact, he became so upset by the revelations that he once again decided that his wife must go away but, before finalizing the arrangements, the Fridays came to see me.

Basically they were both reasonable and pleasant people. They had a modest but well-kept home, teenage daughters who were making good progress, and no serious problems of any kind that affected them. As they both agreed emphatically, they really had 'everything', and the single outstanding difficulty had been Mrs Friday's brief affair and Mr Friday's inability to cope with it.

There was nothing that one could do about the affair itself; it had happened, and nothing could change that. One could, perhaps, look at the reasons for Mrs Friday's infidelity which remained an entirely isolated and in some ways still mysterious event. But since she had put this behind her, and had genuinely striven to set matters right, this problem seemed of less significance than Mr Friday's morbid preoccupation with the episode. Indeed, there was little chance that the marriage could survive this continuous obsessive probing that produced dismay in Mrs Friday and emotional distress in her husband. In short, before any other action could be usefully taken, it would be essential to eliminate discussion and thought of the affair.

Typically, the many individuals to whom such an event has occurred to disturb their relationship, feel that they can never forget or even fully forgive. For many, such betrayal stands forever as a barrier to a full relationship with the offending partner, and often leads to separation and divorce. For some, the affair of a partner is the occasion for counter-measures of the same kind, while others see this as an opportunity for blackmail and exercising a controlling influence. Just how many couples are able to come to a more effective adjustment is not known, but it certainly seems to be rather hard among those seeking counseling to assume a more dispassionate view and Mr Friday's reaction, although rather morbid, is by no means unusual.

In fact, in Mr Friday's case it was possible to teach him to abandon the discussions that were making life a misery for both partners, and this enabled the reconstruction of the essentially good relationship they had previously enjoyed. It is not, of course, that one is saying that such lapses should simply be overlooked or always excused, but that, if the partners sincerely wish for a reconciliation, and the memory of such an event is an outstanding barrier to this aim, then 'forgetting' becomes essential to progress.

Problems in marriage do not always arise from such dramatic incidents, nor are the solutions to the difficulties so accessible, as the following case shows.

Here are two young people, married only 18 months, who seem to have few ideas in common about their relationship. For him, the central idea is of two people sharing everything, being happy in their cosy little home, spending their time working for and dreaming about the new furniture, the house they would move to in time, the children they would have, and so on. Perhaps a slightly romantic view, but certainly sincerely felt by Mr Maynard. His wife, on the other hand, sees marriage as not interfering at all with the life she had led as a single person and, for her, going out every evening and leading an exciting disco-enhanced existence is supremely important. Their expectations of marriage are miles apart and it is hardly surprising that their attempts to impose their own views about how things should be as brought them into conflict. It was quite evident that neither of them had the slightest intention of abandoning their personal view since, to each of them, that view was entirely reasonable. Where there is no willingness to see the alternative point of view, or capacity to put oneself in the position of one's partner and where self-interest is the sole motivating force, there is precious little that can be achieved. In fact, all relationship rescue operations hinge on two important points. First, that the partners clearly perceive that it is in their interests to make a success of things (one would not say they must have a deep affection, since this is far from being possible in many cases at an early stage); second, that they will *both* need to make some changes before the relationship can be made to work satisfactorily.

These are very simple requirements to state, but it is quite clear that they are not things we can always assume to be true of the people involved. In the case of the Fridays, until the couple sought advice, Mr Friday considered it 'natural' that he would need to satisfy himself about every aspect of his wife's infidelity, and failed to detect the transition into morbid obsession. In the case of the Maynards, the perception of a need to change was absent in both partners.

This book is written for those who feel that their relationship is in jeopardy, or feel that it falls unacceptably short of what is needed. It sets out to teach those who want their relationships to continue and to flourish, how to introduce those changes that promote this end. It does not set out to tell couples how to attain perfect contentment in their interactions and, indeed, no such aim would be realistic. But one can say that couples who succeed in introducing changes of the kind described actually *do* find a new level of happiness in their relationship. Much depends on the spirit of compromise that we all need to adopt if we are to solve the problems produced by sharing our lives with someone else. It is quite impossible to solve problems if we approach them in the Maynard spirit and, even if only tentatively held at the outset, the assumption that one could be wrong or that there may be a better way of doing things, must be present.

If you were told that there was a one-in-three chance that you would suffer from some serious disease in the prime of your life, no doubt you would feel dismayed. If you were informed that a major misfortune would happen in the foreseeable future that would cause considerable suffering to you and your family, you

Feeling their relationship falls short of perfection

would be justifiably worried. Yet all of us are now at risk. In the UK, at the time of writing, one marriage in three ends in divorce, and the rate is still increasing. In the USA the rate has already reached the level of one marriage failure out of every two. The problems are not confined to Western Europe and North America, for one-third of all marriages in the Soviet Union also end in divorce – more than 50 per cent of them in the first year.

The tendency to find cause for discontent in the early years is, in fact, well documented. In the UK, for example, the peak divorce rate occurs in the first three years of marriage and, in the USA, it is reported that two out of five divorces occur in the first two years. Such early emergence of problems is often attributed to difficulties in settling down to set rules on such matters as sex, money, comfort, intellectual stimulation, and leisure activities, all of which involve changes from the unrealistic ideas developed during courtship.

Few events in our lives will produce the anguish that goes

with a broken marriage; not only is it a shattering personal experience but it also frequently spells financial hardship, and is the direct cause of great unhappiness and instability for any children of that relationship. One is tempted to wonder whether divorce or separation has been made too easy, and whether all the emphasis has been on ending the misery of the 'unsuited' couple, rather than on attempts to rehabilitate them. Perhaps, it might be thought, some attempt to put things right should be mandatory before divorce can be considered, although this would be of little help to those whose broken relationship is in the context of the now fashionable unmarried state.

Many partners who have suffered separation take comfort in a second relationship, in the form of developing one that has been already started during marriage, or one embarked upon to fill the void created by the breakdown. There is rather bad news for such individuals, since relationship failures appear to increase rather than decrease. The *Soviet Literary Gazette* states that it is not unusual for a woman of 28 to have been married two or three times, which suggests that little can have been learned about how to share one's life if one needs to renew the task so frequently. Indeed, any counselor will testify that most people who embark on the second or third relationship seem not to have formed any coherent and successful strategy of the kind that is needed. When I recently asked a 40-year-old man what had happened to his first two marriages, he could only say 'Well, I suppose someone better came along.'

It *is* possible that we do have an impoverished relationship, or even that there are those among us with whom it is utterly impossible to live. Yet, experience of problems in this area leads one to conclude that such cases are the exception, rather than the rule. In fact, as has been shown, if an advertisement has been placed in a newspaper, asking people to come along and discuss their marriages if they consider them to be satisfying to both partners, they report precisely the same problems as those found in couples seeking marriage guidance. The difference between the groups is almost entirely due to distressed couples making heavy weather of the difficulties. Happily married people see the problems as less severe, whereas the unhappily married see them as more grave.

This kind of difference extends to the individual's perceptior of a partner's behavior. Among the failing marriage group, less than 40 per cent of the behavior of partners is regarded as 'positive' while, for the contented marriage group, the figure is around 60 per cent. In short, the same behavior can be looked on either more or less favorably, according to whether you feel your marriage is good or not. We could begin to believe that getting people either to *think* their marriage is good, or having them see the behavior of their partner differently, might be a good therapy.

On this theme it is useful to note, too, that it is quite simple to identify the couple at risk as they seem to find it absurdly easy to get into conflict over what should be neutral topics. While it is understandable that they can disagree about how to spend money or raise the kids, it is less clear why they can't see eye-to-eye about how sunny it was yesterday!

Going back to the high risk presented by marriage, or to those living together in a close relationship, one is immediately struck by the apparent lack of concern about the hazards involved. Marriage and other forms of long-term relationship seem not to be at all discouraged by the catastrophic outcomes readily apparent to us all, which invites us to ask just why this is so. Certainly, if the risk of a smoker developing lung cancer by the age of 30 was a 50/50 chance, one imagines that there would be fewer cigarettes sold. In fact, increased physical risk *is* involved, since the death rate among the separated, divorced, and widowed is two to three times higher than the average. Among the causes of this increased mortality are more frequent car accidents and suicides, and it is also notable that there is increased alcoholism in these individuals. Why is this kind of statistic not a deterrent to marriage? First, it would appear that many people do not think that divorce will happen to them. There is an awareness of the frequency with which such tragedies happen to others but, somehow, they feel that they will be the lucky ones who manage to stay together.

Second, there is a feeling that we are in control of this area of human relationships in much the same way that one can be said to choose the moment at which to cross the road. But it is very clear that thinking of marriage and other close relationships in this way is gravely mistaken: whether a good or bad thing, the conception of a rather mechanical control over some kind of 'contraption', where one can put on the brakes or step on the gas at will, or as the occasion demands, simply does not apply. The relationship vehicle needs a lot more thought and care than that.

A third problem is that many people enter their relationship without any good idea of what will be needed to sustain it. The early stages of attachment tend to be shrouded in optimism and heavily colored by the pleasant feelings born of enjoyment without responsibility. There is most often only the briefest glimpse of the less satisfactory aspects of life together and overexposure to the nicer situations, out of which arises the delusion that life will simply go on being 'like that' – or might even improve still further with marriage. Some may consider much notions would be best dispelled by 'trial' marriages or 'live-in' relationships, but, judging by the general lack of success that attends such arrangements, perhaps it is better that the individuals concerned did not enter a legally binding contract.

A fourth problem appears to stem from the dangerous assumption that the faults that can be clearly perceived in one's partner can be easily corrected in a closer relationship. Without doubt, it is absurdly naïve to imagine that marriage affords us an opportunity to iron out the faults we can see in our partners, and make them more like . . . well, more like *us*. This book takes a quite different approach to such problems, as will be apparent.

But the staggering increase in marriage failure is probably only in part due to the illusions described so far. An additional factor, for example, is that death during early and middle age is less common, and this alone allows more time to encounter problems and to translate these into divorce action.

A more important cause would seem to be a prevailing social climate that emphasizes rights rather than responsibilities. There is little need to draw attention here to the proliferation of various 'Rights' movements, and to compare this growth of protest to the dearth of 'Responsibilities' groups; even the idea of the latter may, these days, seem to be slightly ridiculous, and the traditional sources of what one would probably call moral teaching have either shifted entirely to the 'Rights' end of the scale, or remain largely silent.

In such a climate, of course, it becomes rather difficult to identify the real causes of social problems, and governments confine their action, largely, to symptomatic treatment. For drug abuse, drug addiction centres are established; for criminal acti ity, larger prisons are constructed; and, for marriage problems, easier divorce laws.

In any event, people with marital problems often spend a considerable time describing how they are deprived of opportunities for self-expression, but much less often seek clarification of how they can better understand their partner and, in general, experience difficulty in seeing the other point of view. Indeed, the language of complaint these days is often that of the various protest groups, and the arguments are presented in the vivid and belligerent manner commonly employed by such groups. It is in this context that one contemplates, with some reservations, legislation that actively supports and encourages the dissolution of relationships which, one must presume, reflects 'popular demand.' At the very least, one might expect that some balance might be introduced which gives appropriate emphasis to social agencies and attitudes which inspire hope that relationships could be improved, as an alternative to being terminated. This is not to say, of course, that social evolution should not take place, nor to deny that there is often a decline in satisfaction with relationships after children have left home, following retirement, or when illness or some other stressful event occurs in the family. Problems arising from such events or changes can markedly increase the sense of stress and strain.

It might also be said that the difficulty with much of the legislation on social issues and problems is the emphasis on immediate outcome. It is self-evident that an aggrieved partner may achieve satisfaction from divorce proceedings, both in material and psychological ways; what is less evident, although more compelling when examined carefully, are the benefits denied to everyone affected by that legal action. In general, it seems that social action and, broadly, social legislation, often fail to examine consequences in any detailed and rational manner, but tend to cater for instant remedies to relieve immediate suffering.

Easier and quicker divorce, it must be said, actually creates a demand for such action and discourages problem-solving by those in marital distress. The more common separations become, the less the stigma attaching to such steps, and the easier it becomes to follow such a course. Furthermore, by exhibiting such model of social behavior to our children, the more likely we ake it that they will copy that behavior.

In fact, far from being surprised that divorce rates show alarming increases, it is a matter that should not raise any eyebrows, and should not be the occasion for blaming 'unemployment' or 'pressure of life' or 'stress of modern living.'

It was pointed out earlier that, where breakdown has occurred, there is a strong tendency to repeat the search for and identification of a suitable partner. This happens despite evidence that, on average, second marriages (excluding those resulting from the death of a partner) are much less successful. There seems to be a marked tendency to establish such bonds with another person despite social pressures that now act against firm relationships. Nevertheless, alternatives to conventional marital arrangements have been devised, and some individuals turn to 'solutions' such as 'open relationships', network marriages, and communal living. There is no evidence whatsoever that any of these alternatives provides a solution to relationship problems but, rather, that they are often a cause of further unhappiness.

Where breakdown has occurred, and a second relationship is in prospect, there is often a blindness to the personal limitations which led to the former outcome – and may do so again with the next partner. A few do attach some culpability to their own shortcomings, but this tends to be a rather partial view and, most often, the break-up is again seen as the other person's fault. The same story is told by both partners, and one is left with the strong impression that both bore some responsibility for what happened, and that neither partner had found a useful way of handling quite ordinary relationship problems. In fact, as pointed out earlier, the difference between failed and successful relationships is not the *number* of problems, but the attitude adopted to difficulties that arise and the willingness to examine solutions other than that of quitting.

At this point, one must recognize the partners in a failing relationship protest that they *have* tried, over long periods of time, but they simply *can't* get their partner to *see* that he (or she) ought to change. In fact, typically, the couple in difficulties are locked into their own hurt and their own view of things, and a vital first step to reconciliation is to have them recognize that an alternative view is needed, and that others, facing similar problems, manage to find effective ways of dealing with them.

It may take a little time to have the couple recognize that theiproblems are not unique and that a different spirit and approach will be needed. It is certainly not easy to accept this kind of 'arbitration' attitude when one feels, very strongly, that one's partner is so clearly at fault, and that this ought to be very obvious to even the most casual observer. Patiently bringing the client to that fresh appreciation is helped when specific problems are examined, for it is here that the kind of global accusations that tend to be made can be trimmed down to more sensible dimensions.

For example, it is quite possible for a wife to call her husband 'completely selfish' (and it could be true!) until we examine the detail of his behavior and find that he has shown consideration in some cases. Perhaps, in some situations, he has been completely unselfish. It may suit the husband with relationship problems to label his wife 'completely neurotic' but, when her behavior is looked at more closely, it is invariably the case that he has to agree she isn't always perverse and irrational.

The focus, as these introductory remarks indicate, is on the precise nature of the things that are causing the problems and the construction of some means of overcoming them. Most of us have the capacity to do this and, by and large, circumstances would allow us to do so if only we had a framework for tackling difficulties and bringing them under control.

This book sets out to provide that framework by describing just how the distressed couple should analyze their difficulties, and how they should deal with them. It is assumed that they will have a genuine desire to stay together, and that they only require someone to show how this can be achieved.

Those with severe marital problems will have often despaired of 'trying' any more; rows and conflict will have been commonplace, and blame, doubt, lack of trust, and abusive exchanges will have been part and parcel of everyday existence. For these individuals the effort to introduce changes will be more difficult, and progress may be painfully slow but, even in the most troubled cases, the effort made can be both highly successful and infinitely rewarding.

For those who merely sense that all is not quite as it should be in their relationship, the task of bringing about change, a closer understanding, and greater fulfilment, will be easier and quicker. They will find the rules given in this book simpler to apply, and

KEEF

Rows and conflict have been commonplace

rapidly develop a capacity for communication and other skills that can greatly enhance their lives together.

As for the rules themselves, these are basically simple to understand and the problems lie largely in remembering to apply them, or feeling that one wants to do so. Learning how to really listen to your partner, learning how to tackle disagreements, how to arrive at sound joint decision-making plans, and how to get rid of old verbal habits, are all important. So, too, are developing a respect for your partner, setting aside pride and hurt feelings, and learning to live in the present rather than in the past. In fact, every aspect of your life together should be touched by these rules.

Generally, the distressed couple will experience doubts about making changes and whether or not simple step-by-step improvements will be enough to save a marriage where 'everything is wrong.' Patience is needed, as the necessary changes are not going to be made overnight, but perseverance and effort can produce a surprising amount of progress.

The partners following the program described in this book must be prepared for the inevitable disappointments and difficulties that will occur. Although the rules are easy to understand, they will not always be observed by one or other partner on some occasions; in these circumstances it is tempting for the other partner to feel let down, that all the effort is one-sided, and so on. This temptation has to be resisted and the problems that arise, and which must be anticipated as quite natural, are to be seen as only temporary setbacks, to be tackled and overcome.

Finally, when changes in behavior are first introduced there is a feeling of awkwardness as well as the idea of 'you go first.' Where the former is concerned, the uncomfortable feeling about doing something in a contrived way, just because the program tells you to, will soon pass. In fact, because you gain by the things your partner does for you, it becomes a pleasant thing, rather than a chore, to make the changes. Be patient and wait for the slight awkwardness to pass.

So far as the second point is concerned, it is vital that the partners do not wait for each other to make the first move. Each will learn what changes they are to make and must get on with that task, not waiting for the other to begin the business of changing. The temptation to feel that the problems are really all the fault of the other person, and that he (or she) must be the first to show willingness to make amends, must be set aside as damaging to the program and to the relationship.

SUMMARY

Sweeping social changes have affected marriage and other close relationships. Plain 'economic sense' no longer serves to sustain marriage now that women have become important contributors to family finances, and we are exposed to intense pressures from changing ideas about sexual freedom and independence. Husbands are no longer evaluated simply as breadwinners, but as companions and lovers, and many of us have great difficulty in coming to terms with such fundamental changes. There is, furthermore, a new kind of impatience in the search for satisfaction, there is less willingness to spend time putting things right, and relationships that 'don't work' are abandoned in favor of some alternative that seems to offer a cure for unhappiness.

Divorce or separation is a catastrophe for most people. Unhappiness and health hazard statistics are a reflection of the strain of broken relationships, the financial cost can be ruinous, and children of the marriage suffer both immediately and later in life.

New relationships that may be formed are, statistically, even less likely to succeed, and often fail to confer the happiness sought at such heavy cost. Yet marriage remains by far the most popular form of voluntary institution, with well over 90 per cent of us choosing to live out our lives in such a relationship. Indeed, the need to share our lives with others is so compelling that, despite the trauma of divorce, the majority will choose to repeat the experience or turn to some alternative, such as the live-in relationship, open marriage, or communal living. There is no evidence whatsoever that these alternatives provide the solution to relationship problems, and much that would remind us that they are frequently the source of further unhappiness.

The decision to stay together is not easy to take, and is even harder to translate into an enduring and satisfying relationship. Most couples will need guidance and help to do so, since there is no clear idea of why things have gone so wrong, nor does a marital crisis provide insight into how things may be put right.

Both partners must appreciate that changes are needed, and both must be prepared to undertake these changes without waiting for the other to make the first move. A desire to make the relationship work is crucial and the partners must show willingness and patience to work to that end.

CHAPTER 2

Agreeing a Plan for Change

Emmie had kept the incriminating letters Tom had written during his affair. She didn't quite know why, but told herself that she would hang on to them just in case they came in useful. She and Tom had made a tentative start to rebuilding their own relationship but, as she would often point out, how could she trust him again after what had happened? For his part, Tom had agreed to end the affair with June, but he felt he ought to make contact with her by occasional letters and telephone calls because 'you just can't walk out of someone's life like that.' In short, both kept some important part of their problem alive by their actions; neither felt able simply to write off the past or to show complete trust and faith in a new beginning, and they spent a lot of time carefully circling around each other, warily watching for more signs of disharmony.

What Emmie should do is burn the letters as a measure of the trust and commitment she is prepared to give to the fresh start. What Tom should do is simply stop writing and telephoning which, apart from upsetting Emmie, is really a way of keeping in touch in case he needs to revive the old friendship.

Maybe you are not precisely in the same situation as Emmie or Tom, but a token of our earnest intentions is called for whenever we decide to stay together. Sometimes this may be only a small sacrifice – in a sense – but it may be of considerable importance to our partner. He (or she) may just want to be offered lips to kiss on parting in the morning, or on greeting in the evening as a change from the brief and obviously chilly presentation of a cheek to 'peck.' Maybe she (or he) still wishes to show by this coldness that 'I'm still mad about what you did and can't bring myself to show any warmth,' but it is behavior that could well be changed (and is not impossible to change) if this is the token of earnest required by the partner.

But before we consider how we may start to identify the changes in behavior that we should make, let us begin by taking stock of our motivation to change. In other words, we must ask the question, do we want to really try to make the relationship work?

The following table lists the kind of ideas that should occur to us when asking ourselves just how seriously committed we are to starting again. Be absolutely truthful about your answers – there is no point at all in fooling yourself about these matters. Don't worry too much if your honest answers show that you have a long way to go, but be encouraged about the future of your relationship if you and your partner can both say 'yes' to most of the items. Don't argue about how you and your partner fill in your answers to the questions, simply see them as an honest assessment of how each of you feels at the moment and, should there be a lot of 'no' answers, look at this as your target when you get around to evaluating how things have changed one month from now.

HAVE YOU THE BASIC COMMITMENT TO CHANGE?

	SHE		HE	
	YES	NO	YES	NO
1. I would really like to stay with my partner.	☐	☐	☐	☐
2. I am willing to do what I can to improve my relationship.	☐	☐	☐	☐
3. I am optimistic that we can make a success of things if we try hard enough.	☐	☐	☐	☐
4. I would like to get to know how to start putting things right between us.	☐	☐	☐	☐
5. We need some help to make our relationship better than it is.	☐	☐	☐	☐
6. I really want to give more if I know my partner wants this too.	☐	☐	☐	☐
7. I accept that the way things are is the responsibility of both of us and we both need to change.	☐	☐	☐	☐
8. I can clearly see that by making changes we will both be very much happier.	☐	☐	☐	☐
9. I am ready to make a start on improving my relationship and quite prepared to show my commitment by making an immediate change to my behavior.	☐	☐	☐	☐
10. I am ready to forget past mistakes and concentrate on our future together.	☐	☐	☐	☐
11. I accept that to make all the changes needed will take time, but I am prepared to work patiently to this end.	☐	☐	☐	☐
12. I appreciate that there will still be problems to face but I will try to deal with them and try not to get discouraged if we don't solve them at once.	☐	☐	☐	☐

The next step in our program for change is achieved by drawing up a contract between yourselves which sets out as clearly as possible what your joint major objectives will be. It isn't a binding legal document, of course, but it should be taken seriously since this kind of solemn pledge to acknowledge your commitment to change acts as an important incentive. We are less ready to do things blatantly against the terms of such an understanding if we have put our intentions down on paper and have added our names to it. In fact this kind of declaration has been found to have very useful results in many different problem situations. So, go ahead and complete the contract set out below, and make sure you look at it several times each week to remind yourselves of your obligations.

CONTRACT

We . . . . (she) and . . . . (he) have both decided to improve our relationship and in order to do so we have jointly agreed to:
1. Read the program for change that is described in this book.
2. Do our level best to put into practice the kind of rules described.
3. Take all the steps described to collect and evaluate information about each other so that we can become more aware of our own and our partner's viewpoint.
4. Do our best to make the changes in our behaviour and attitude that the program demands.

Signed .... (she)

.... (he)

Date ....

There is, by the way, nothing phoney about having a contract, nor about the 'forced' changes in your own behavior that you will make. It may *feel* odd, strange, contrived, or foolish, but *it works* and that is the only thing that really matters right now.

Understandably, there will be some differences of opinion about whether or not one or other partner has dishonored the contract. You must deal with these as indicated in subsequent

Making a contract

chapters and **most certainly must not:**

1. Be insincere by trying to cover up your failure to live up to the contract.
2. Get embroiled in a fight or argument about who did what.

Rather, **you must:**

1. Be honest in admitting when you have failed to do what you said you would.
2. Sit down with your partner and, in the proper spirit of good relations, discuss *what* went wrong, *why* it went wrong, and *how* it can be put right in the future.

One of the basic problems of distressed couples is that of discouraging the rather global 'dismissive' terms they tend to use quite automatically. Unreasonable, untrue, or at least very unconstructive generalizations are the basic stuff of a failing relationship, and it is quite hard for the partners concerned to stop using these statements and concentrate on employing more helpful strategies. Good examples of the kind of comments to avoid are readily available but, to remind you, here are some common ones:

'You simply can't reason with her at all . . . she's just a hopeless neurotic . . .'
'He's impossible . . . utterly selfish and always will be . . . just like his father (mother, etc.).'

These are quite satisfying brickbats to throw when one is feeling thoroughly angry and upset: they express utter contempt and the notion that one is dealing with incurable conditions. After all, the 'hopeless neurotic' can't change, and the entire blame for everything that goes wrong is due to this condition. It leaves no need at all for *him* to try a little harder. Similarly, anyone who is 'impossible' and 'utterly selfish' can't be changed by anything or anyone, so we needn't try at all. The trouble with such statements is that they are invariably untrue (or only true in parts), they alienate rather than bring people closer and, most importantly, they totally fail to lead to any constructive course of action.

The contract strictly rules out such comments, which the couple must strive to eliminate from their exchanges with each other. But they must also pay attention to another use of language which, while pretending to be quite an innocent description, expresses a very negative attitude toward the partner. A couple of examples will illustrate this.

A client describing her husband's poor sexual performance said 'You see doctor (gesturing appropriately to specific parts of her husband's anatomy) he's just like a wet lettuce.' She had really set out to describe his difficulty in getting an erection, but couldn't restrain herself from giving insult to her husband while doing so. Certainly, the problem is not helped by such descriptions and, more likely, they actually get in the way of solution.

In another case a husband, entering a room where a number of other husbands and wives were gathered, exclaimed loudly to his wife 'You don't look quite as "with it" as the others but I bet they can't cook like you.' The statement could possibly be true – and would probably be more painful for his wife to hear if it was – but it should not have been made. Such backhanded compliments, when challenged, often lead to two kinds of defensive reactions. One is a heated denial that any offense was given or intended, and the other is to admit what was said, but to argue that it was only a joke and call the offended person 'far too sensitive.'

The distressed couple must work hard to eliminate these remarks which, as was pointed out in the first chapter, have really become a bad habit. Don't find yourself using them but, if you do slip up, be honest by admitting your mistake.

Another kind of problem about keeping to the contract arises when we find that we really haven't made a firm commitment to our partner, or we are still undecided about what we want to do. For example, Joe may drink excessively and Jane makes it clear that this has to stop or she is leaving. On this basis Joe may cut down on his drinking and completely avoid being the drunken nuisance that Jane complains about but, instead of acknowledging his efforts, she may begin to argue that the change has come too late. It is very hard, now, for Joe to know what he can do to win Jane's approval and create a better relationship.

In another example, Louise has agreed to make a better job of keeping the house tidy, and in fact does make an effort to do so. She's proud of what she has achieved in this way and feels that Roy should notice the change, but he still comes home and starts to tidy up the hall, undermining her confidence about making changes in the future.

It should be apparent now that the basis of the programe for improving relationships is to make changes in our behavior. To some, simply to say that this is what one is offering as a solution to their problems, will appear as quite unworkable. After all, they will point out, I don't *feel* like making the change requested, but when I feel better about my partner I'll certainly be happy to do it! Understandably, many individuals would put things this way around and, of course, we are much more used to the idea of doing things for people we love, and who have done nothing to offend us; we are certainly not used to the notion of setting out to give to those with whom we are angry or who, in our view, have given us nothing for so long. Yet, it is undeniably the case that, by changing our own behavior, we not only set in motion a whole train of further changes in ourselves and others, but that our *feelings* begin to change too.

Think, for example, of the man who believes that all French people are intensely nationalistic and full of ideas about their superiority. When that person meets a French girl who is attrac-

tive and vivacious, with whom he falls in love, and who recipro-
cates all those feelings, then he can quite easily begin to see that
French people are not all self-centered and superior. In fact, all
the evidence that has been gathered on this point bears out the
conclusion that the more we test out our convictions about the
world, the more disposed we are to make some changes to our
viewpoint. It is quite possible to go on, for example, hating all
Germans and all Japanese so long as we insulate ourselves from
direct experience of them. Making the effort to meet them,
socialize with them, and so on, affects our prejudice, even if at
first this is a rather grudging admission that people of these
nationalities are, basically, not very different from ourselves.

I am not suggesting, of course, that all our ideas and convictions should be changed, nor that all of them are quite baseless.
Anyone who has been in a Japanese prisoner-of-war camp can
dispute our notions that hatreds are unjustified and without
foundation. What is wrong and counter-productive for
ourselves, is to *continue* to behave as if we can only live in the past,
with all the strong emotions and reactions that belong to another
time and a totally different situation.

The strong emotions that affect the couple in distress are a
good example of tendencies to fight and re-fight old battles, to
keep a fresh memory of insults received and wounds sustained
over the years, and allow such recollections to continue to affect
our approach to the partnership. It is essential to make some
changes that will put an end to such a state of affairs; we must
resolve to break the chain, and be ready to test out new ways of
behaving and looking at our relationships. All the evidence
points to this effort bringing greater satisfaction and increased
happiness to couples, but simply resolving to change can be only
as successful as our New Year resolutions, unless we have a
systematic and considered attack upon the problem.

START BY MAKING SMALL CHANGES

One of the most basic rules is to begin with a few easy-to-change
ways rather than those which are entrenched and more difficult.
It goes without saying that, at first, couples have a reluctance to
give too much and, as often as not, feel that it is the other person
who should be doing the giving. So, big changes are not likely to

be supported by strong motivation and, because they are not easily achieved, can produce discouragement early in the program. Making small and easily produced changes provides speedy evidence of success and encouragement for the partners to make further efforts.

ACCENTUATE THE POSITIVE

'I wish you wouldn't', or 'why do you always', are familiar beginnings to gripes and complaints in relationships. We are for ever hoping, it seems, that other people would just get rid of their imperfections and, if they managed to do so, why, life would be very much happier! It will be quite obvious that, to the partner who is the target of the complaint, such 'moans' don't just have a familiar ring, but have become tedious and inspire feelings of resentment rather than eagerness to comply with whatever is implied. Far better is to put the change in a positive form so that, for example, it is better to say, 'I would like you to fold up the newspaper and put it on the table, please,' than 'why do you always leave the newspaper spread out all over the floor and just walk off, leaving me to tidy up?' Or, 'I'd like you to put your arms round me and kiss me more often,' rather than 'you never seem to show any affection for me.'

While the whole world doesn't change because you have put your wishes in a positive rather than negative form, it should be obvious that the recipient will feel better about it that way. If the object of communication has been simply to wound your partner, or 'get at' him or her, then the negative form is very successful. But, if the object is to inform about your real feelings, and to be precise about what you would like to happen, then the positive form is by far the better way.

BE PRECISE

Saying just what you mean has often become a lost art among distressed couples who spend so much of their communication effort in finding indirect or 'coded' ways of expressing anger and resentment. In these exchanges very little knowledge is gained about precisely what behavior would be acceptable; the nearest the couple come to doing this is in global statements about 'being closer', 'less selfish', and so on. An important part of our program is concerned with trying to identify some *particular* change that should take place in your partner's behavior, and this is discussed in the next chapter. However, for now it may simply be said that it is unhelpful to Roger to know that Hazel would like him to make himself more useful in the house; rather, she must tell him just what jobs she would like him to do. Why? Because Hazel has pretty definite ideas about what is *her* work and what is his. She would like him to help with the washing up, she wants him to fix the shelf and the fuses, she would like him to bathe the kids or read them a story; but she doesn't want him to use the vacuum cleaner, make the beds or to cook because, in her eyes, these are important to her role as a woman and housewife. Any attempt on Roger's part to 'help out' by trying to bake a cake would be seen by Hazel as interference. However well intentioned he might be, she could easily 'decide' to take this action as a challenge to her role, or an oblique reference to her being an inferior cook.

So the rule is to be quite specific about what it is **you** want to happen. Once you get into the habit of doing this it really is quite easy and successful.

SET A NUMBER OF TARGET CHANGES

In the beginning, just to get the feel of making changes, you should set one or two quite simple targets for change. As the idea of making changes becomes easier and more familiar, it becomes possible to speed up the process. Indeed, it is a good idea to set a manageable number of changes in process since the more rapid progress helps to keep up the motivation of both partners. As in so many areas of psychological endeavor, early enthusiasm can quite quickly fade, and the small changes that looked so significant at first can come to seem rather trivial and are less remarkable.

Each week the couple should decide upon the changes and exchanges that they will make in that period. The exact number doesn't matter particularly, but the target should be set at something that will be clear evidence of progress made, but not so great that the partners lose track of what was agreed, or that failures to achieve target become frequent. The latter will, of course, lead to discouragement and opting out. If you are affected by these factors, then look to see if you are not setting your sights a bit too high and need to revise your list of changes to make success easier to attain.

REMEMBER YOUR SUCCESSES

The adage that nothing succeeds like success is as true of relationships as of any other aspect of human functioning. But sometimes our efforts – and real progress made – tend to be overshadowed by the things that remain to be done, so keeping a record of achievement is very important to remind us of what we are doing, why we are doing it, and how far we are 'on target.'

Fred and Monica were on their third week of the program. They had each managed to make some small but important changes in accordance with the rules but Monica, impatient to get to what she thought of as the most important goal of 'feeling secure and really loved', complained about this lack. For her, progress toward her own rather vaguely defined goal was too slow and not clearly related to what she wanted to feel.

Monica could appreciate that Fred had made an effort, and that he was now doing some things that she'd been nagging him about for a long time. He was taking greater care about tidiness, folding his clothes up neatly, putting his tools away after using them, and keeping his cigarette ash in the ash tray. He was more talkative, too, spending two or three hours each week, as agreed, telling her about what he had done at work, and listening to her when she talked about things that had happened in her day. All these agreed changes *had* taken place but Monica hadn't yet got the feeling of being 'secure and really loved.'

In this example, Monica is being impatient and expecting too much too soon, but she is also missing the important point of the program. The feelings of love, security, and respect that the adjusted couple experience, are simply the by-product of putting into practice all the elements of the program. They do communicate well, they do find time to listen, they handle differences of opinion and decision-making in an acceptable way, and so on. In short, the adjusted couple have achieved their happy state by doing all the things that the program advises – they do them quite naturally, while the distressed couple are simply having to learn a somewhat slow and sometimes labored way. Furthermore, couple in difficulties are not just starting the learning process

Keeping a record of progress

from scratch, but having to overcome many negative habits of thought and action before they can introduce the beneficial changes that will be needed.

Monica needs to be reminded at this critical stage to appreciate not only the progress that has been made, but also of the real importance such progress will have for the achievement of her main ambition for the relationship.

WHAT TO DO IF THE CHANGE DIDN'T HAPPEN

In a way Fred and Monica were lucky: the changes they had contracted to make actually were taking place, and progress was being made. For Linda and Tony, however, the two weeks since entering the contract had been 'an absolute failure', according them. The fault didn't lie in setting too many targets for chan or absurdly unrealistic goals but, rather, in their grudging attitude to change. Instead of a proper commitment and determination to stick to their agreement, both had made rather tentative and half-hearted gestures, leaving plenty of opportunity for each to accuse the other of 'backsliding', 'falling down on promises', 'dodging the issues', and the like. Instead of sitting down to examine in a calm and sensible way just what was going wrong, they became locked in conflict about their problems.

It should be clearly understood, right from the beginning, that things rarely go exactly as one would wish, and that there will be many opportunities to pounce upon and punish one's partner for falling short of perfection. What each partner is committed to is really *trying to make the changes work*, not guaranteeing to be 100 per cent successful.

Sometimes partners, like Linda and Tony, fail to really try to fulfil their agreement and get down to tackling the problems. Instead, they turn to their old and dismal failure of a strategy, punishing each other in acrimonious exchanges, tracing the perceived defects of character to respective mothers and fathers, and generally engaging in quite fruitless and damaging warfare.

If the changes do not occur as planned, then there are certain steps that must be taken. You are not being asked to overlook the fact that your partner failed to live up to the agreement, but you *are* being required to examine the lapse in a particular way. First, wait for an appropriate moment – don't simply try to get the matter settled then and there. Sit down together and, in a calm way, go over the particular incident where the agreed changes did not take place. Don't start by being anxious to deny the omission, be quite ready to listen sympathetically to how you may have missed out on some agreed behavior. The aims of the discussion are to be quite clear about the behavior in question (precisely what *didn't* happen), *when* this occurred and exactly what *should* have happened to satisfy your partner. Be ready to concede that you may have missed out on some agreed change if this is the case but, if you are the partner bringing up the omission, then be fair and balanced in your comments. Remember that this is an opportunity to create a better understanding between you, and a more successful relationship generally; *it is* *a trial* of your partner or an opportunity to settle old scores.

KEEP A RECORD OF PROGRESS

It is well known that keeping a record of progress made can be an important motivator. If you can see that the number of changes – each of them requested by you and met by your partner – increases week by week, it becomes an important reminder of achievement. Sometimes, when small changes are being made, it is easy to lose sight of the improvement trend. So a record of these changes can be useful both in keeping our motivation up to scratch as well as a permanent reminder of the alterations in behavior that we must go on making. A simple check-list is usually all that is needed, the changes being recorded as they are agreed, and a tick made against them every week as they are kept and added to, as in the example below:

HE AGREES TO

	Week		
	1	2	3 etc.
1.			
2.			
3.			
4.			
5.			
etc.			

SHE AGREES TO

	Week		
	1	2	3 etc.
1.			
2.			
3.			
4.			
5.			
etc.			

SUMMARY OF THE MAIN POINTS IN THIS CHAPTER

1. A contract helps to firm-up our commitment to making the necessary changes.

2. Don't expect the contract to make change easy – there *will* be problems and misunderstandings.

3. When problems arise don't try to solve them in the old ways but, rather, set aside time to discuss how they arose and how they can be avoided in future.

4. Don't wait for your partner to make the first move; be ready to make changes and ensure that *you* meet the agreement made. We tend to be afraid to make changes in case we are let down; don't allow this worry to interfere with your determination to make the relationship work.

5. Begin by agreeing upon small changes to be made. Don't try anything too ambitious at first – enjoy the success you can obtain without too much effort.

6. Each week, if you have met your agreed targets, go on to make further changes. Don't allow yourself to get stuck just completing a few easy-to-make changes and failing to go on to more important and fundamental matters.

7. The changes you agree to make should be positive so that you are asking someone to *do something* rather than to *stop doing something*.

CHAPTER 3

How to Diagnose your Problem, and more about Making Changes

We all, from time to time, tune in to our personal dreams of a world that is just the way we would want it to be. It is clear that our close relationships fall short of what our fantasies tell us would be perfection, where everything happens just the way it should. But we can usually see that this paradise is only a reflection of what *we* want, rather than what would be perfection in the eyes of other, including our partners, and that we are really taking a rather one-sided view of things. In fact, it is reasonable to take the attitude that the important objective in our relationships is to strike a balance between what we want and what our partners want; having things just *my* way is a recipe for difficulties and, in any case, is unrealistic. Recognizing this, we can sometimes comfort ourselves with the thought that it would be a dull life without a few differences.

Of course, for the distressed couple, the reality of their relationship falls far short of the tolerable, let alone the ideal. The differences between them in attitude and behavior appear as unbridgeable chasms. Each partner has usually retreated into their respective bunker, firing shots at the 'enemy', but with only a very limited view of what is going on from their defensive entrenchment.

Getting out of those positions is not easy. Typically, each sees the other as mainly responsible for any difficulties and, at the most, all they have done is defend themselves. Progress i⸱

creating a better life together will depend crucially on shedding the defenses, abandoning our attacks on our partner, and agreeing that both will need to change. Understandly, at first each will see change as necessary in the other person and not in themselves; after all, he (or she) really caused it all by . . .

It is useful, at this stage, to try to examine the width of the gulf that exists and, accordingly, the couple should complete the following listing. If your score is a good one – in the sense that you haven't checked many negative statements as 'true' – then your problems might be easy to deal with. But, if your score is a bad one, the task will be that much harder, although not to be thought of as hopeless. Be encouraged if you check items 10, 13, 16, 21, 23, 28, and 31 as 'true.'

Although you may check many negatives in the 'How Serious is Your Relationship Problem' scale, you will almost certainly find that your answers have been something of an overstatement or exaggeration. The way we feel tends to color our judgment, and when we feel pretty low in spirits we are inclined to see everything in a bad light omitting, perhaps, those things that don't fit our generally gloomy view.

HOW SERIOUS IS YOUR RELATIONSHIP PROBLEM?

	True	Untrue

1. I am very unhappy the way things are ....
2. We have far too many fights ....
3. Small things that go wrong always lead to big conflicts ....
4. One or other of us has left home for a period to 'cool off' ....
5. We seem to take an opposite point of view about almost everything ....
6. We have had reconciliations, but they never last very long ....
7. Things between us have grown steadily worse...
8. Many things about my partner seem to irritate me ....
9. We seem to have little or nothing in common
10. We do have some pleasant moments together ....
11. We are temperamentally unsuited..............
12. There is a lack of trust between us ....
13. We can agree on some things.....................
14. It is difficult to 'get together' socially, workwise, or in any other way ....
15. All the good has gone from our relationship
16. I still have some respect for my partner ....
17. My partner is the main cause of our problems ....
18. My partner lacks respect for me or what I do
19. My partner takes everything I say or do the wrong way ....
20. I don't understand my partner...................

	True	Untrue
21. I think my partner is basically a good person		
22. I do not feel loved or wanted		
23. There are moments of real affection		
24. Even small things easily get out of perspective		
25. I'm just waiting for the moment to leave		
26. We always punish, insult, and put each other down		
27. Old resentments come up again and again ...		
28. My partner has some good points..............		
29. My partner never tells me anything		
30. When I try to make an effort it is ignored		
31. At least we don't have too many fights.........		

For example, Vera and Jim had been having a lot of difficulties and, over the past year or two, had grown further and further apart. One of Vera's main complaints was about Jim's meanness and resentment that she spent money on things *he* felt were not absolutely necessary but which, to Vera, were essentials, such as cosmetics. The arguments about expenditure were made much worse when Jim lost his job and, according to Vera, he became totally obsessed about money. In fact, from her point of view, Jim was now a complete miser and 'wouldn't spend a penny if he could help it.'

It was certainly true that Jim had always been careful and disliked borrowing; indeed, he had always avoided buying on instalments, preferring to save up for the things they needed. No doubt, too, that Jim's concern about money was greatly increased by losing his job, although he could not be described as miserly or obsessed by money. Vera, in short, took a very real issue, but distorted it considerably because it touched upon matters that were very important to her, namely her appearance.

Because we tend to introduce such distortions into our perceptions of other people, it is sometimes helpful to keep a running check on the nice and nasty things that your partner does. This counteracts the tendency to draw the general conclusion that he or she is *completely* something or other. It would have been quite easy for Vera to see that Jim is not watching every penny in the way she states, if she had noted how he seems to find a little pocket money for the children, or a few flowers for his mother's grave. Basically, the problem is not one of his total obsession with money, but one of how each of the partners looks at the way that the money they have should be spent. Maybe Jim's problem is not miserliness but, rather, a tendency to think that he should be the judge of where the money goes – he thinks that his way of doing things is only common sense, but this isn't at all Vera's notion of what is reasonable. Somehow, these two views are never discussed in a sensible way and, so far as Jim is concerned, Vera is a spendthrift and, where Vera is concerned, Jim stays a tightwad. Neither position is true but the couple have no good idea how to get out of the polarized positions they have adopted.

DON'T GENERALIZE

The first thing to realize is that problems must be put into a concrete form so that the real nature of the differences between the partners can be properly appreciated. Most often such differences have been stated in a form both general and difficult to contradict. For example, Vera frequently talks about Jim as 'just impossible to live with', while he refers to her as 'totally irrational.' These generalizations are not only inaccurate but really don't allow scope for them to be challenged, and certainly don't enable one's partner to see any action to take to avoid being labeled 'impossible' or 'irrational.' The unwanted statements come in many different forms ('he *never* listens', 'she's completely selfish', 'he's totally neurotic', 'she's just hopeless', and so on) and all of them antagonize and alienate rather than help matters.

BE SPECIFIC

So, the couple must learn to avoid these generalities and to make their requests for change in very specific terms. For example, when you fill in the form on p. 38, which tries to identify six things you would like your partner to do more often, you must avoid saying 'be nicer' or 'try to be less difficult' and, instead, focus on the things that would actually contribute in some way to *being* 'nicer' or 'less difficult.' The kind of things to bear in mind are, for example:

> 'Kiss me goodbye before leaving for work.'
> 'Bring me flowers sometimes.'
> 'Help Peter with his homework.'
> 'Offer to make the supper.'
> 'Bring me a cup of tea in bed sometimes.'
> 'Tell me I look nice.'
> 'Make some food you know I like best.'
> 'Buy tickets for a show.'
> 'Take me out for a meal on occasions.'
> 'Offer to return my books to the library.'
> 'Offer your lips to be kissed instead of a cheek.'
> 'Spend a half hour helping me with this chore.'
> 'Say you enjoyed the meal I cooked.'
> 'Hold hands while watching TV.'

These are quite specific actions or words which allow very little scope for misunderstanding. Your partner, to whom such requests are directed, will understand very well what is being asked. Furthermore, such changes are (intentionally) not at all difficult to provide by a reasonably compliant partner and may, in fact, tend to seem slightly trivial when first mentioned. How can such small changes be helpful, it may be asked, when the relationship is in such disrepair?

The answer is quite simple and straightforward. Even small changes begin to reverse the pattern of destructive interpersonal actions. Indeed, it is often the case that the welter of small things 'going wrong' has been the cause of major problems and 'global' accusations, such as 'You don't care' or 'I'm just taken for granted.' Small changes *can* and *do* lead to a general revision of behavior and attitudes.

FROM NEGATIVE TO POSITIVE

Distressed couples generally have fallen into the habit of being accusatory and fault-finding; they rarely see or comment on the better things that each does, but are all too ready to appreciate the less pleasant aspects. The changes you are to make in your behavior should be a reflection of this willingness to be more positive about your needs and what you want your partner to do. To help you to see this more clearly, look at the following list of negative and positive ways of putting the same point.

Negative	*Positive*
1. You never tell me how nice I look.	1. I'd like you to tell me I look nice sometimes.
2. You never touch me or kiss me except when you want sex.	2. I want you to touch and kiss me more often – just being loving.
3. You never ask me how my day went.	3. Ask me how my day went.
4. You won't do any of the jobs I ask you to do.	4. Please put the shelf up this weekend.
5. You keep spending without a thought for the bank balance.	5. Let's sit down together and look at what we spend.
6. You always spring plans you've made at the last moment.	6. I would like you to tell me about things so I've got time to prepare.
7. You're always getting upset if I talk to someone else at a party.	7. I'd like to be able to talk to someone of the opposite sex without you being jealous.
8. You don't do enough to keep the house clean.	8. Tell me how I can help you to keep the house tidy.
9. You never help out with all the work I have to do.	9. I'd like to have you help me more with . . .
10. You're always too busy to talk to me.	10. I'd like you to spend some time each week just talking to me.

You will appreciate how much better we can respond to someone who makes a positive request than to someone who accuses us of falling down on what we should be doing. Putting things posi·

Holding hands while watching TV

tively also gives a clearer idea of what it is that would be an improvement. For example, 'You don't do any of the jobs I ask you to do' is much more ambiguous than simply asking someone to put up the shelf, clear out the garage, or mend the fence.

Although the couple in trouble may argue that they *have* asked for those specific things, again and again, without anything being done, it is a very different matter if the request is part of a deal that we are making with our partner.

Putting matters in simple positive terms also reduces the possibility of misunderstandings and misinterpretations that are the common currency of the troubled relationship. Lena, for example, told Neil that he looked really worn out, and he concluded that she meant he was getting to look old and unattractive. Dennis told Phyllis that he was a bit tired and didn't feel too much like making love, and she concluded that he meant he didn't care about her any more. In fact, in many cases, it has become difficult to say or do anything that is going to be taken at face value, and a totally new approach is needed to communication. The way in which this is done is set out in a later chapter.

A further problem raised by couples in distress is that the changes are not real – not *from the heart*, so to speak. It is true that they are requested and, to an extent, are contrived. There is a certain awkwardness at first in producing them 'to order', but this soon disappears and the new words and actions become natural, habitual, and acceptable. The natural reluctance, for example, of the 'wronged' wife to kiss her husband on the lips and respond warmly to him, can be a little hard for her to overcome. She should not be too disappointed if the feelings that would ordinarily accompany such actions simply aren't experienced; a bit of patience is needed, allowing time for the natural feelings to come back, and assisting the return of the feelings **by the actions themselves**.

Use the answers that you have selected on the following scale as the basis for making the changes that are needed. These should, of course, be small, reasonable, and affect your partner's behavior and attitudes. It may not be reasonable, for example, to suggest that you should have twice the amount of money to spend on clothes; although this *is* a specific change, it is unreasonable if it brings into question weighty matters about the family budget. It would be fine, on the other hand, to negotiate a 'clothes allowance' at some time if this has been a cause of disagreement in the past. The important thing at the outset is to keep the changes small, meaningful and quite simple to arrange.

I would like my partner to make the following six changes. (Be absolutely specific)

He	She
1.	1. ....
2.	2. ....
3.	3. ....
4.	4. ....
5.	5. ....
6.	6. ....

MAKING THE TRADE

Now, at this stage, compare your lists and decide, through discussion, which of the changes you will select to make in the first week. Choose about three or four of them which seem – to both of you – to be good exchanges. For example:

Bob agrees to help tidy up after supper and Jenny agrees that she will keep a record of shopping expenditure.

Fiona will put her arms around Colin and kiss him warmly, both when he leaves for the office and when he gets home again while, each weekend, he will do one of the jobs he has been putting off.

Dawn will write a letter inviting Ken's mother for the weekend, and he will telephone the newsagent to complain about the bill.

Stan agrees to be responsible for keeping all the household accounts in order, and Mary agrees to get the kids bathed and ready for bed in good time every night.

DON'T ARGUE ABOUT THE CHANGES

The discussions in which you plan the changes you want to bring about, and any modifications you agree, must be amicable. If the requests are reasonable and small, then there shouldn't be too much difficulty. But a common complaint is that the behavior in question is there already – it is just that one's partner never sees it or admits to it being present.

It is the responsibility of both partners to take the requested change seriously, and not to argue about it. It is essential to assume that your partner is sincere about the matter and, if the change is asked for, it is your job to make it – or to make it more evident that you really *are* complying with what is being asked. This is *really* a very fundamental issue, since many couples find a new source of disagreement when specifying changes, arguing that the trade asked for is unfair or bogus. Simply accept the requested change at its face value and get on with making it.

GIVE TO GET

Essentially, then, the task is to identify those specific words or ctions you want from your partner and trade 'this for that.' rget any idea that this is a bit like bazaar bargaining and so is the product of 'true love' and 'respect'; the happiest couple would not survive long if they did not give to each other and get from each other. The difference is that, in your case, as partners in a failing or difficult relationship, the changes and exchanges need to be made more deliberately before they can become a natural part of your everyday behavior.

EXTEND THE LIST OF CHANGES

The six changes noted already are only a beginning and, week by week, more will need to be added to the list. A bit of soul-searching can be quite useful in getting a clearer idea of what needs to be done, so the following type of listing can be added.

I would like to make the following changes to my own behavior (Be specific)

He	She
1.	1. ....
2.	2. ....
3.	3. ....
4.	4. ....
etc.	etc.

It will be obvious that seeing our own faults, as opposed to having them pointed out to us, can assist our determination to change. Again, such resolutions should be kept simple, positive, and specific, so that what is needed is self-evident and practical. Examples are:

'I will spend more time playing football with Johnnie.'
'I will make a special effort with the cooking on one day each week.'
'I will make conversation instead of looking at TV.'
'I will make a point of saying something nice to my partner every day.'

We tend to feel that we are too busy to play football with the kids, there is no time to cook that special meal, too tired in the evening to do other than slump in front of TV, or that we can't be bothered to say nice things. But we all know that these are really quit small matters that could easily be arranged if we wished to do s

COMMON PROBLEMS CHECKLIST

The specific changes that need to take place in your own relationship may well be quite unique. These are the lists that you will be working with, trading the changes made in your negotiations with each other, and gradually extending the list week by week.

On the other hand, there are quite a few common problems that distressed couples have and it is worth offering a list of these for you to examine. They tend to be a bit more general in nature than the specific changes on which you will be mainly concentrating, so it is necessary, as you will see, to 'back up' the general point with specific courses of action to be taken. Here are some of these general points:

I would like my partner to be:	He wants	She wants
1. More ready to say 'sorry'	....	....
2. Less moody	....	....
3. Less inclined to 'flare up'	....	....
4. Avoid long periods of 'not speaking'	....	....
5. More ready to 'laugh things off'	....	....
6. Less inclined to take things the wrong way	....	....
7. More trusting	....	....
8. More understanding	....	....
9. More sensitive to how I feel	....	....
10. More ambitious	....	....
11. More generous	....	....
12. More relaxed about things	....	....
13. More interested in his/her appearance	....	....
14. More interested in cultural/ intellectual pursuits	....	....
15. More interested in outdoor/sporting activities	....	....
More interested in social activities	....	....

	He wants	She wants
17. More affectionate	....	....
18. More ready to share	....	....
19. More ready to forgive and forget	....	....
20. More exciting	....	....

Being ready to say 'Sorry'

You may be able to add quite a lot of additional items to this list, and this is a useful exercise, but these are really of little use unless they are put into a positive form and unless you can quite clearly identify a course of action that would really *change* things. The following examples illustrate this point.

Being 'more understanding' is often a code to cover those things that one's partner expects us to do when he or she 'down', has had a bad time of it, or feels tired and overwhelmed by events. Being 'understanding' here can mean simply being sympathetic, putting arms around one's partner and just getting physically close. It could mean sitting down to go through what has been bothering your partner and helping to solve the problem or come to terms with it. In fact, one really doesn't know just what is meant until it has been well discussed.

Being 'more generous' can simply reflect her view that she tends to feel guilty when she buys anything for herself, or that he feels she is too mean in putting on a good 'spread' when his parents come to stay.

Being 'more affectionate' for him may mean that he wants his partner to be more active and responsive in sex; for her it may mean that he should show kindness and attention at times other than when he wants sex.

In short, these general statements need to be put into quite concrete terms to show our partners what it is we want and just what kind of actions or words would meet our requirements. So, there is another list to make for use together with the general points, which will look something like this:

Write down three ways in which your partner could show:

1. More readiness to say 'sorry'.
2. Less inclination to 'flare up'.

and so on.

Once again, it is important to stress that people with relationship problems seem to prefer to keep their complaints to global ones. When they do this it gives them the impression of being in the right, but it is hard for their partners to get to grips with what is required. This kind of lofty generalization also encourages our partners to adopt the same way of behaving or speaking, and so we become further and further away from a meaningful exchange of just what is wrong and what we can do to put it right. Problem solving can only take place when we can see what the problem is.

One further comment can be made about the common problems list. You may well find that both of you want to make the same general point, each feeling that the other needs to be more ready to say sorry, less ready to flare up, and so on. This should alert you to the deceptive nature of putting things in a global form, allowing you each to see the same fault in the other. Sometimes, when the difficulty is examined closely, it turns out to involve faults that the couple share.

Robert and Lucy each felt that the other was disinclined to spend more time together, each was being selfish in doing their own thing and being neglectful of the interests and needs of the other. In fact, both spent a good deal of spare time on matters of interest to themselves alone, Robert spending as much time as he could on the golf course or in the clubhouse, while Lucy spent whatever time she could in the garden. He felt she could take golf lessons or at least join him in more social events in the clubhouse; she felt, quite rightly, that he left her to do everything in the garden without lifting a finger to help. Both, in a sense, were right about their complaints, but they had failed to do anything constructive about the problem, each feeling the other should be the one to change. In this case both needed to make changes, he to do a bit more with Lucy in the garden, and she to show more readiness to be part of his golfing world.

On the other hand, it is sometimes found that the general point is difficult to sustain by pointing to particular examples of things to change. In such cases the generalization has become a kind of verbal smokescreen behind which the individual hides, and which simply serves the purpose of keeping alive differences and antagonisms. We can all appreciate this type of reaction in industrial disputes, where there is deliberate recourse to allegations of 'provocative behavior', or 'refusal to engage in meaningful discussions', by the other party, but it is more difficult to identify such mechanisms in ourselves.

Elizabeth stated flatly that John didn't show a readiness to 'share' but, when asked to specify how this was known to her, couldn't think of any examples. Nevertheless, she continued to assert that it was true, even if she couldn't think just then of how John showed such tendencies. Steve was categorical that Maureen 'could be more trusting', but was unable to give any good examples of this. In fact, Steve could only cite a rather weak instance of what could have been a reasonable doubt in Maureen's mind, dating from five years earlier.

In short, challenging the general assertion that there is a major problem lurking around, which quite ruins the relationship, is important in two ways. Firstly, we can discover more precisely what is bothering our partner and, secondly, we can sometimes come to realize that the problem has no real basis in fact. Of course, in this latter case, it does not mean that no problems exist, but that we have failed to identify them in a way that is helpful.

PROBLEMS, PROBLEMS

Making changes, even when you have decided to adopt the rules set out in this book, is by no means easy. Invariably, both partners feel hurt and not listened to, and both are firmly convinced that their particular point of view is not understood. Jane felt badly let down by Roger, believing that he left her to take care of everything at home, and gave her no support at all with the domestic crises that seemed to hit her all too often. Roger, for his part, was frankly astonished that Jane didn't appreciate that he was working these long hours and being away from home so much, simply for the sake of all the family. He thinks 'If only she could see all the strain I've been going through, the sacrifices I've made for all of us . . . as if I'm actually *enjoying* it!' Jane could say precisely the same.

Maybe they get around to talking about their problems but they soon get back to accusations and recriminations of this kind:

'I remember when you used to say . . .'
'You've changed a lot since we first met . . .'
'You promised me . . .'
'What's the good of talking, all I get is . . .'
'I'm just sick of you, life, the kids and everything.'

In fact nothing very constructive happens in their discussions but a good deal is happening to help them to drift further apart. By and large, their failing strategies fall into the following categories:

1. *Denigration* – e.g. 'You just can't seem to stick at anything', or 'You're just idle.'
2. *Threats* – e.g. 'I'm really not sure I can stay with you', or 'I'm going to do something pretty drastic about this . . .'
3. *Old Battlegrounds* – e.g. 'I can still remember very well when you . . .', or 'You're a fine one to talk when you . . .'
4. *Insinuation* – e.g. in the form of affected vagueness, 'You're behaving rather strangely lately . . .', or 'Are you feeling quite well?'

The couple must come to realize that these strategies are failing either to change the partner or to provide any real satisfactions, and that a new approach is needed.

SUMMARY OF THE POINTS IN THIS CHAPTER

1. We have to recognize that good relationships are those which balance our own views with those of our partner. *My way*, as an ideal for each partner, is a recipe for disaster.
2. The changes to be made must be undertaken by both partners.
3. Learn to express your need for change positively – don't ask your partner to *stop* doing something, but to *begin* to do something.
4. Don't put the request for change in general terms, make it very specific. Don't ask your partner to 'be nicer'; decide what you mean by this and ask him or her to show this *specific* behavior.
5. Create a list of the changes you want your partner to make and see how you can reach agreement on an exchange.
6. Don't be too ambitious at first. Be content to have a few changes made of a simple kind, and add to the list as you go along.
7. Don't argue about the exchanges. Be prepared to accept your partner's assessment of what you need to do and try hard to make it a habit.
8. Try to cut out all denigration and punishment of your partner. Don't raise old arguments, and cut out the little 'digs' at your partner made in affected innocence.

CHAPTER 4

Talking, Listening, and Showing How You Feel

At the first interview with Mr and Mrs Richards, it is glaringly obvious that any semblance of effective communication between them is totally absent. The session degenerates into the kind of slanging match that has served as their style of verbal contact for many months, despite the strenuous efforts of the interviewer to create a more constructive dialog. Any marriage counselor can testify to the difficulty that is so often found in breaking through the rancor and ill-will, trying to get the partners to see another side to the story, and preventing the session becoming just another opportunity for airing grievances rather than solving problems.

On this particular occasion Mr Richards makes a feeble attempt to keep to the ground rules set out by the interviewer. Mrs Richards, now in unstoppable form, simply seizes on her husband's attempt at compliance as yet another deception of the kind he has always shown. 'Oh yes, doctor, he can turn on the charm when he wants to . . . he's always been able to do that and a lot of people believe him and think it's me in the wrong . . . you should just see him, though, when we're out of this room . . .,' and so on. Her husband's own efforts to engage in more constructive examination of the problem are punctuated by lengthy explanations of why 'out of sheer self-defence' he has had to resort to some of the things she claims he does. They make a sorry sight, this angry couple with their sense of personal outrage and their absolute insistence on being the victim of unfair treatment. Whatever foolish act or hurtful word is uttered by each, is defended vehemently as entirely justified by the behavior of the partner. Indeed, the mildest suggestion by the interviewer that a more balanced view may be needed is sometimes met with increased outrage that anyone should fail to see that it is *his* (or her) fault.

In a sense, the past is quite irrelevant to the problems facing this couple, although both of them seem to want to live out the past, to put things right that they see have gone wrong, to punish the one who inflicted misery, to 'understand' just why this or that happened. In fact, a frequent complaint is that 'I just don't understand how he (she) could have done it . . . I just want to know *why*,' but it is clear that the understanding required doesn't involve an explanation which apportions some responsibility to both partners. 'I want to know *why*' only means 'I want your sympathy and backing for *my* way of seeing things, and your agreement that my partner is the guilty party.' In this sense, going into the past, trying to sort out who did what, to whom and why, is a waste of time, even if one could sort out the complexities of long ago. The only real answer to the problem is to set about the construction of a future for the couple which *does* meet their needs and wants.

But before they have any chance at all of creating a better relationship, they must learn to communicate effectively. Indeed, the mastery of interpersonal communication is crucial. Basically, this involves getting rid of destructive verbal and non-verbal habits and substituting constructive ones. *Out* must go character assassinations, insults, wild assertions, overgeneralizations, perpetual complaints and gripes, while *in* must come keeping to the facts, sticking to the issue in question, and showing genuine concern for the wellbeing of one's partner.

At first sight the task looks too intimidating and the destructive exchanges too fixed to be modified. But some quite simple strategies can bring out very important changes in just a short time. It may seem that saying 'Tell me how you got along today' instead of 'Do you realize what a hell of a time I've had . . .,' or simply a grunt and retreat behind your newspaper, is a very small change. But it can have profound effects on your partner and begin a process of changes that extend to all aspects of your life.

'You relax while I bath the kids'

It may appear irrelevant to the problems in your relationship to substitute 'OK . . . you relax, it won't take me long to give the kids their bath', for 'Don't you think I've got enough to do without coming home to this . . .', but the effect of doing so can go well beyond the bit of self-sacrifice involved.

In part, our 'instinct' to react badly instead of well in our close relationships is deeply ingrained. We wouldn't dream of offering the rudeness and offensive comments to neighbors that we inflict on our partners in life. Few of us would want to say 'My God, you look awful in that dress' to our neighbor's wife, but we can say it more freely to our own. Rarely are we tempted to tell a friend that he might stand a bit closer to the deodorant spray, but telling a husband this doesn't pose any serious problem. In fact, practically the only people who say insulting or wounding things to us are our own family.

To an extent this reflects a feeling of security; we can say these things to our partners and get away with it whereas, if said to a friend or stranger, we might get a punch on the nose.

But the tendency to act badly rather than well by couples in distress is often due to quite different causes. It is the unwillingness to 'give an inch' to one's partner, to punish for misdeeds, to 'put down', and generally act destructively toward someone held to be 'responsible for everything that's going wrong.' It isn't our feelings of security that lead to such utterances, but our feelings of *hurt* and *insecurity*. Furthermore, the 'offensive' remark tends to be the only kind that is given by the partners in distress; in contrast, for those getting on well together, there are plenty of positive comments and actions. Remember, too, the verbal part of the message is given a special meaning by the body language we use and, in the case of distressed couples, it is this non-verbal communication that gives a sharper point to the words uttered.

In every act of communication there are two components we must keep in mind: the content of the message and the feeling behind what is said. For example, it is obvious that we can use the words 'I need help' in several different ways. We can, if we choose, use the words as a humble request for assistance, or they can be said in a manner that suggests 'I'd like to have help from anyone but you, in fact I need help *about* you.' 'Remember that you promised David to take him to the football match' can be a simple reminder, a concerned request to make sure you leave plenty of time to deal with the matter, or a brickbat for someone who never keeps a promise.

In any event, couples in distress don't manage a proper exchange of ideas and opinions, they fail to use the words and non-verbal signs that would be helpful, they inject spite into every aspect of their interaction, and square up to each other, defensively or belligerently, at the drop of a hat. Typical of such failure of communication is the exchange of views between Bob and Julie. Bob started out by wanting to talk about the recent bank statement, but it all went very wrong:

Bob: 'I just opened this bank statement and it looks like bad news . . .'

Julie: 'I've told you many times that you have to give me an idea of how much I can spend.'

Bob: 'You've got a nerve, why I've told you time and again about your overspending.'

Julie: 'You certainly go on bitching about how much *I* spend . . . what about your new car . . .'

Bob: 'Typical, just like you to bring that in, you know damn well we just couldn't go on with that old car.'

Julie: 'Well, you said you'd deal with all the bills, so don't complain when you get it wrong.'

Bob: 'For God's sake, you never listen to a thing I tell you . . . it's just no use talking to you.'

Not only have they allowed the problem to become a highly emotive business – and turned what might have been a useful discussion into a battleground – but they have quite forgotten about the statement itself and what it contained.

Recognizing what they are doing is quite hard for Bob and Julie; they've come to regard these exchanges as 'normal' and think it quite typical of the *other person* to turn everything into a row. Each could turn in triumph to an onlooker and claim, 'You see how he/she is?', fully convinced that they have been unjustly victimized by the other.

Simply realizing how they have both been responsible (often, a tape recording of these exchanges can have a salutory effect) doesn't confer any special ability to re-run the communication any better; the habits and skills are simply not there to be used in their *own* exchanges, although they may be very well preserved in their conversations and interactions with other people.

RULES FOR GOOD COMMUNICATION

It has been pointed out already that most communication involves both verbal and non-verbal information. The former obviously consists of the words we choose to convey messages, and the latter consists of all the ways, other than words, that add meaning to what we say. For example, saying 'I love you' in a rather absent-minded way while keeping one eye on the football results is quite a different matter from using the same words while holding hands and looking into someone's eyes. Our posture, the tone of voice we use, the physical proximity to our partner, and so on, all help to convey the message. Our job in learning to communicate effectively is to use both words and non-verbal signals in the right way.

Good communication depends on the content of the message, which means keeping out irrelevances, putting messages across in a positive way, and by all other means ensuring that the right kind of reception is secured for the message transmitted.

Choosing the right words

Sometimes counselors have clients play a game, in which they are set the task of discussing some 'neutral' topic, such as the holiday they would most like to have, or the pleasures of the countryside. Of course, distressed couples find it hard to avoid drifting into offensive comment, accusations, dragging in irrelevant references to shortcoming of the past, and so on. The counselor's job is to keep a count of the number of such 'failures', sometimes using counters to give and take away points. Couples can be very surprised to have this kind of feedback about how far they have fallen short of being effective communicators and, in particular, how often they manage to choose the 'wrong' rather than the 'right' word or phrase.

TALK POSITIVELY

Talking positively is the first thing to learn and is helped if we can begin to recognize some of the faults that reflect negative talk. Here, for example, are some of the *irrelevant negatives* that we might get rid of as 'starters' to our messages:

'I know you think my ideas are always stupid, but . . .'
'Of course, you've never really liked my family, but . . .'
'You have to realize that I'm doing too much, but . . .'
'I know I'm not important to you, but . . .'
'I suppose you'll accuse me of being jealous, but . . .'
'You'll get upset when I mention this, but . . .'
'You always accuse me of being insensitive, but . . .'

'I realize how hard you work, but a lot of time is wasted in . . .'

Talking positively is definitely not helped by such introductions – they simply focus the mind of the receiver on the need to be on guard and ready to reject whatever the next bit of the message is to be. The change that must take place is that of *leaving out the negative introduction*; think positively about the essential message you wish to convey, and give only that. So, if you really wish to talk about selling the house and moving to a smaller one, don't introduce the topic by saying 'I know you think my ideas are stupid', or by any other negative 'lead-in.' Rather, say 'I want to talk about selling this house and maybe moving to a smaller one.'

If what you really want to say is that you've invited your parents to stay next weekend, just say that, rather than introduce it by, 'You'll get upset when I mention this.' You *don't* know how your partner will react but you will certainly help him or her to decide by using negative starters.

You will need practice in changing these habits and, remember, such negatives can be introduced not just at the very beginning, but can be repeatedly slipped into any part of the communication. Be vigilant: set yourself the task of monitoring your 'negatives' and try to reduce the number of times you make this mistake. If you catch yourself using them, just stop, apologize, and start all over again. You will be pleasantly surprised how much a bit of determination to succeed can do to get rid of a bad verbal habit.

AVOID THE FINAL NEGATIVE

A similar fault is that of introducing the final negative. Statements that begin quite well are spoiled by this kind of thing, some examples of which are:

'I don't mind giving you a hand with making the beds . . . you seem to need a fair amount of help these days.'

'OK, I'll giver the kids their bath . . . but I hope you realize I'm just as bushed as you are.'

'Thanks for ringing my folks . . . the trouble is you picked just the wrong time.'

'That was really a great meal . . . just a pity about letting the potatoes burn.'

'Well, you really look good in that outfit . . . once you get rid of that nasty-looking spot.'

Distressed couples spend a lot of time, when they are really trying quite hard to be nice, ruining the good bits with an unpleasant ending to the statement. These endings have to be eliminated, even though it may be true that your partner asks for more help, doesn't see how tired *you* are, picks the wrong time to phone, burns the potatoes, or has a facial blemish. Getting someone on *your* side, making your partner *feel* good, and responding to you positively, means keeping to the positive comment. Just leave it that it was a great meal, or a marvellous idea to phone. There's no need for the negative – it adds nothing to the basic message – and it actually spoils all the positive part of what you wanted to say. In fact, it's worse, since your message lifts up only to put down, and makes your partner feel it's really no good trying – whatever he or she does, it won't be right. It discourages, sours, and must be cut out.

Simply getting to know what you are doing in this respect, and making sure you monitor your performance, will improve things greatly. You will notice that the word 'but' keeps appearing in these spoiled positive comments, and just keeping an eye on the use of this little word can help to eliminate the unwanted negative. 'You did a great job of decorating . . . but you left the kitchen in a hell of a mess', or 'Thanks for putting up the shelves . . . pity about them being tilted to the right', are no way to reward effort. The kitchen *may* have been left in a mess, and the shelves rather lop-sided, but the jobs *were* done, and recognition of an *unspoiled* kind should be given.

BE HONEST — BUT TACTFULLY

What has been said above may give the impression that you are never to raise the least objection to things that go wrong. You must, it may be thought, swallow the burned potatoes without comment, cope with the sloping shelf without complaint, and so on. There are, in fact, many occasions where it really is better to say nothing at all, simply because the matter is too trivial to risk creating problems. The odd newspaper left on the floor instead of being cleaned up, the occasion when there's too much salt in the cooking or the pastry went wrong, and similar events, simply aren't worth making waves. But the serious and persistent problems *do* need our attention and must be dealt with in formal discussions, as described in Chapter 3. It is on such formal occasions that we need to choose our words with great care, but it is also true that we will need to exercise the came degree of care during our more casual conversations of the kind just described. In fact, there will be a number of specific situations in which you will feel the need to bring your partner's attention to some behavior that you would like to be changed, but it hasn't yet been part of a formal agreement.

Susan and Guy were driving home one evening from dinner with friends. They were a bit later than intended and Guy, driving too fast, went into a skid as he took a corner. Susan, always nervous about driving fast, became very upset and began shouting at Guy, 'For God's sake, you're going to kill us both . . . you're a lousy, reckless, crazy driver.' She had been nervous, right from the beginning of the journey, but had kept silent until the car began to slide which, quite suddenly, triggered off all her pent-up anxieties. Guy, feeling guilty about his driving error and upset by Susan's outburst, began to attack her and decided against slowing down to prove how silly the whole thing was, and that he wasn't going to be cowed into crawling along just to pacify a 'neurotic' woman.

We can see how both are wrong in what they do and say, but the situation began with poor communication long before the skid happened. What Susan *should* have said at the start of the journey was, 'When I'm in the car with you and you drive fast, I get really scared. Would you mind going a bit slower so I don't get so upset, please?' This allows Guy to be compliant and considerate. He can now respond by saying, 'Well, I guess we'd better arrive in one piece, and I expect the baby sitter won't mind us being a few minutes later than we said.'

In short, Susan can be honest and tell Guy what she feels; she doesn't have to just sit there and put up with the situation, but she *does* have an obligation to put her point well. The words she chooses and the timing of what she says can be a great improvement over her outburst. They don't have to get into combat about the problem and become polarized by adopting emotional extremes.

The reason why Susan doesn't raise the matter earlier is interesting. She *does* feel apprehensive, and sits in the passenger seat feeling tense and strained. In fact, in the last few minutes of the dinner party, she had already begun to think of the journey home and to dread it. Susan, like many who have communication problems, isn't just worried to drive home with Guy, she also worries about what Guy will think and say if he's challenged about anything. Because they don't communicate well, any direct expression of feelings is seen as likely to cause more problems. She may think:

'It was a good evening . . . I mustn't spoil it now by saying something he won't want to hear.'

'If I say anything, I'll just get too upset and lose control . . . maybe I'd better keep quiet.'

'We're getting on a bit better at the moment . . . I'll try not to say anything to spoil things between us.'

'I know we end up shouting if I make any criticism . . . it's just not worth rocking the boat.'

'If I complain about his driving, he'll simply think I'm a weak and neurotic person.'

It is true that when Susan has tackled Guy in the past about such things the problem has been made worse rather than better. His experience of trying to get Susan to see *his* point of view has had much the same outcome. Their attempts at honest revelations have never worked well because they have tended to 'catastrophize' (i.e. to think this will lead to disagreement and rows), and so have only allowed their feelings to surface in an explosive manner. Usually, over the months or years, such explosions have become easier to arrive at and have become the *only* way of communicating ideas that have an emotional loading.

They must learn that it is possible to express feelings in an honest way without catastrophic results. But, it is also necessary to exercise tact in making these revelations of personal feelings, whether in your formal agreements to change or in more 'casual' communication. The topic of honesty is raised again in the chapters on conflict management, decision-making, and stress, but we must note that, although revelations can be helpful, *brutal* honesty can be destructive.

TALK AS IF YOU CARE

When couples are first asked to make changes, there may be two quite typical reactions. First, they feel (despite a partial willingness to try again) that they don't *really want* to be nice to their partners. Second, they feel that, if they do change their approach, it will look foolish and seem contrived to their partner. It has to be recognized that both influences are there for most couples in distress but, nevertheless, they must try to make the changes in order to achieve progress in becoming more 'natural' and to enjoy producing the changes. At first, the couple simply have to accept that what *feels and is* rather forced will become easy, effortless, and profitable with just a little practice.

We must help this process along by whatever means we can. Changes made with very obvious lack of enthusiasm and a show of only grudging acquiescence will be less successful. It has already been pointed out that the varying tones of voice used in conjunction with the same verbal message produce very different reactions in the listener. By and large, the rule is that we avoid a 'negative' voice and use a 'positive' tone for our interactions with partners. The following list will help you to identify these, but maybe your partner can (honestly, but tactfully) put you on the right tracks if you are in doubt.

Positive voice	*Negative voice*
Warm, affectionate	Impatient, irritable
Lower in tone	'Clipped', harsh
Soft, tender	Hurt, whining
Happy, laughing	
	Angry, sarcastic
Concerned, caring	Tense, frightened
Cheerful, bubbly	Cold, hard

All your contacts and attempts to communicate with your partner should be a reflection of the positive list. Some of these qualities are a bit easier to produce at first than are others; for example, 'bright cheerfulness' may be simpler to manage than 'warm, affectionate'. The latter becomes easier as the partnership moves along in the pattern of change and as you get to feel more comfortable, allowing the deeper feelings to show. Confidence comes, too, when your partner is reciprocating, and you can see it's not just a solo effort. Just as important, of course, is to eliminate as much of the negative tone as you possibly can. On balance, you can be sure that positive output by you will bring positive reactions from your partners; negative output will have just the opposite effect.

Although punishment, harshness, and anger can have an effect on the behavior of others, the influence tends to be deterrent rather than creating the warm feelings we would like to inspire in our relationships. Couples in distress have resorted to punishment and anger because they feel they have exhausted all the positive ways of doing things, but they are usually wrong about this, or have tried to be 'nice' in an unsystematic way. Anyone who keeps a record of the different outcomes that can be achieved by using positive and negative voice tones will quickly appreciate the difference. Don't think that simply using the former will lead to you getting your own way – indeed, that would be entirely the wrong approach to the situation. What you are aiming for is a better understanding of your partner, a greater sharing of viewpoints, and the support and affection that comes in a good relationship. Being positive is not a subtle weapon in a war you are waging, but an olive branch that can bring many benefits to both you and your partner.

USE POSITIVE FACIAL EXPRESSIONS

Some more non-verbal rules

We have talked about more effective choice of the words you use and the tone of voice you employ. The latter is a non-verbal 'signal' in the sense that it is not words but some influence upon those words. But other non-verbal signals will help you to convey your message effectively and assist in developing the closer relationship and changes that you and your partner are looking for. Your face is all important cue to how your message will be received and the rule, once more, is to be facially positive, not negative. To help you with this, look at the following list:

Positive expression	*Negative expression*
Smiling	Frowning
Laughing	Looking angry, glaring
Nodding head	Disgusted expression
Eyebrows raised a little	Crying
Looking sympathetic	Smirking, mocking
Looking tender	Fearful, anxious
Mouth corners up a little	Shaking head, sighing
	Compressed lips
	Eyes rolled up

These positive facial expressions are all usually well rehearsed and we certainly haven't forgotten about them. Rather, it is a matter of no longer using them, or making little use of them, in our interactions with our partners. When they are added to the rules already given, conflicts will become less frequent and agreements made much easier, but a *conscious* attempt to make ourselves employ these useful aids is needed.

POSITIVE BODY CUES

Everyone has heard of 'body language' and how we show the way we feel by using parts of our body rather than words. Our faces and voice tones are part of this communication process, but we can also convey quite a lot to our partner through the general bodily postures we adopt. Once more, the rule is to use positive rather than negative cues to make the right kind of impact on our partners. Here are lists to help you to do this.

Positive body cues	*Negative body cues*
Touching (affectionately)	Holding body tense
Being attentive	Spreading hands in disgust
Looking relaxed	Gestures of contempt
Leaning forward	Pointing, jabbing finger
Being physically close	Folded arms
Eye contact	Turning away
Open arms	Keeping at a distance
Remain still	Agitated movement

KEEF

Maintaining eye contact

It is not at all surprising, when interviewing a distressed couple, to see how they tend to sit apart, turn their heads so that they don't need to look at each other directly, hold themselves taut, use gestures of despair and dismissal, and so on. In these ways they convey, without the need for words, the view they have of their relationship. These bodily cues, too, need to be changed at the same time as changes are introduced in other areas of communication. Practice is, as usual, an important element in change, and it is necessary to remain alert and conscious of what is required if success is to be achieved.

A SIMPLE PACKAGE

Although it is important to include as many of the rules referred to as you possibly can, there is a simple 'package' of communication aids that can be helpful right from the start. There are seven easy points to remember and, if you put them into practice, you should see an immediate change for the better in communication with your partner.

These points are:

1. Keep eye contact as much as possible. Don't look down or away from your partner.
2. Stand (or sit) still. Don't keep shifting your position or moving around.
3. Get parity of status. Both sit, or both stand, so one of you isn't looking up and the other looking down.
4. Get close. Be as physically close as you can manage and, if possible, be in physical contact, for example holding hands.
5. Don't ramble in your talk, try not to have too many pauses, gaps, and 'fillers', such as 'er'.
6. Speak in a concerned way, let your voice, facial expression, and body posture convey all the positive feelings you can muster.
7. Choose your words carefully. Be positive in what you say; cut out the negatives.
8. Try writing down the things you want to say to help you to talk more easily.

Jeff is a fine example of bad communication. When he gets home in the evening he doesn't say 'hello' (he may grunt a recognition if he happens to bump into Louise), but goes straight into the living room, switches on the TV, and hides behind the paper. He is in his 'impregnable' mood and it would take a brave woman to try and break into these defences. When Louise tries to do this Jeff is given to heavy sighs, eyes rolling upwards, snorts of derision, sometimes eyes closed in a 'long-suffering' manner and, on occasion, loud tuneless humming, as if to drown out the thing he doesn't want to hear. In fact, he a very good communicator, in a sense; he wants Louise to know that he has had quite enough, he simply doesn't want to know, and will become resistant if she tries to force him.

If Jeff wished to do so, and if only he knew how, he could produce the kind of reactions in Louise that even he would admit were nice for him. He could, for example, stop rushing around the house at times, showing exaggerated activity, plumping up the cushions, sighing heavily as he clears up the kids' toys and, in every other way, telling Louise 'look what you make me do . . . work you should have got on with before I came home . . . this isn't my job, what kind of home is it that you run . . . we should be eating right now instead of having to start cleaning the house.'

But Louise can communicate too. She can sometimes manage to tuck the baby under one arm and use the vacuum cleaner with the other, finding this most effective in the living room where Jeff is watching TV with one eye and his newspaper with the other. Louise wishes Jeff to know what absolute hell it is to have *her* lot in life.

It would be so easy – apart from his 'natural' resistance to do anything of the sort – for Jeff to come in, say 'Hi', put his arms round Louise and ask her how her day was. He could ask if she could use a little help, talk to her while he's slicing the vegetables, squat down with the baby and play a little, and so on. The actual physical effort involved is small but, for Jeff, the psychological effort is big and, what is more, he doesn't really know what it is that he should be doing. He only knows it's a mess and he just wants out; his thoughts turn repeatedly to how he came to get trapped in this way, and of escape to an altogether better world.

Jeff learned only slowly how his communication was wrong and how to put it right; but he did learn and the big surprise for him was that he really enjoyed the changes in himself. For her part, Louise was adaptable enough to stop her own bad habits just as quickly as Jeff introduced his own changes.

GOOD COMMUNICATION MEANS LISTENING

Couples having problems are generally bad listeners. For one thing they feel they know what answers their partners will give, so they don't need to listen to what the other has to say and, in any case, it is *their* point of view that needs to be heard. They listen with impatience, if they listen at all. Change means actually hearing a partner out, and letting him or her really say what they want the other to hear.

DON'T INTERRUPT

Interruptions are very frequent in such couples' discussions. The need to qualify, amend, and put the other person right is uppermost, rather than patient listening.

Nick and Sally, during their first interview, haven't heard about the interruption rule. Nick starts to answer the interviewer's questions about what changes he might want Sally to make, saying that he'd like her to try to be ready when they have to go out or have the neighbors round. She simply can't bear this charge – which she thinks absolutely untrue – and even if it is true sometimes, well, it's because he leaves her to do everything, so there's always a rush. Her interruption makes Nick frustrated and they fall into the familiar pattern of charge and counter-charge, dragging in their favorite example to support their own views. Even if Nick's story is only partly true, it is what he *feels* to be the case and he must be heard out. Sally's job is to understand how he feels about it – actually to *listen* to what he has to say. Sally needs to be understood, too; maybe Nick's problem is that he needs to make a change in his behavior and help her more so that she can avoid being late. We cannot analyze a problem that is only half understood, nor can people find a solution to their problem unless they give each other some kind of chance to say what they feel is wrong. A little patience by both Sally and Nick, a little real listening, and they will soon find that they can arrive at the kind of agreement that gives Sally some help and spares Nick the frustration of waiting for her to be ready.

OPENING YOUR 'FILTER'

A further difficulty is that, even when partners do 'talk' about things, they seem to use a kind of filter which allows them to hear only what supports their own way of seeing things. In the main they hear the negative part of the message only, or they give the message from their partner a negative interpretation. There are many examples of this, and the following two will serve to make the point.

Judith asks Lennie to remember to order the flowers for her mother's grave, because they left it too late last year to get the kind they wanted. Lennie hears only the 'left it too late' part and, concentrating only on this, gets into a fight about whose fault this was. He has stopped paying attention to, or has 'filtered out', the kind of message that Judith is passing, namely that she wants to remember her mother in the nicest way possible.

Frank, trying to explain to Maureen about the extra work that is going to make him late home, says 'I can't make it back in time to say goodnight to the kids . . . but at least there's the compensation that we're going to talk about the new contract over a good meal.' Maureen doesn't hear this as an apology for being late and as Frank's way of saying 'I'd rather kiss the kids goodnight than have a good meal.' She sees it simply as Frank being late again and enjoying a better meal than they'll have at home.

Listening, *really* listening, will allow you to hear just what it is that your partner is saying and, later in this chapter, there are some instructions on how to get a clearer idea of what your partner means or meant to say.

AVOIDING MIND-READING

A problem in some ways related to what has just been said about 'filtering', is that of mind-reading. The attitude of many distressed couples is that they know perfectly well what is in the mind of their partners – and usually it isn't very nice. Sometimes they take the view 'My partner should know quite well what it is that I want and, if he (she) doesn't know what he (she) *should* be doing, it's no good.' 'Knowing' what is in your partner's mind, without asking, requires you to be a clairvoyant; expecting him or her to know what is in *your* mind requires a mind-reading act by them. Clearly, it is unreasonable to have such expectations, and they don't come from careful thought about the matter, but from bitterness and other unpleasant origins. In any case, it will be obvious that, if both partners have such unrealistic notions, effective communication cannot take place.

Carl and Lena read each other's minds all the time. Whatever Carl says, Lena 'knows' that there is a hidden message behind it of an unpleasant kind. Carl, too, 'knows' what Lena is up to when she makes her innocent remarks; behind them is the kind of rebuke and resentment that she feels for him. Both also 'know' quite well that the other fully appreciates what is needed or, if they didn't, well they damned well should. Carl and Lena, even in their earliest days of marriage, some 10 years ago, have never really tried to talk to each other about their ideas and feelings, have never set aside time just to talk, and almost certainly have little understanding of each other's needs and wants. As changes have taken place to each of them, and within each of them, over the years the need for understanding has grown greater, rather than less, and they have become progressively more isolated by their lack of knowledge of how to communicate. Carl and Lena are novices in this fundamental skill, and they will have to grasp the need for communication as well as setting out to develop some aptitude in that respect.

DELIBERATE MISUNDERSTANDING

A problem familiar to all of us, but especially frequent in the distressed marriage, is the deliberate misunderstanding.

Donald came home after a bad day at work, walked into the kitchen and found the table covered in discarded cut-outs abandoned by the kids, and the floor littered with toys. He pitched into the children about the state of the house, and demanded an instant clean-up. Amy mildly pointed out that he seemed to be a bit grouchy, but Donald would have none of this, hotly denying that he was at all upset, and justifying his bad temper by saying that Amy has failed to bring up the kids properly. Donald knows quite well that his mood has led him to make a big fuss about a small thing and to turn it into an attack on Amy's competence, but he's certainly not going to admit that!

If Donald only stopped to think, he could claim Amy's undivided attention and tell her about his bad day; or even, if he could bring himself just to apologize for blowing up in the way he did, things would improve. As it is, Donald has got used to the idea of putting the blame for how he feels on to the family, and lacks confidence in Amy's willingness to listen and comfort.

HOW TO LISTEN WELL

The recognition of one's communication faults and, in particular, failures to listen properly, is a good start to making changes. Reading the foregoing list of problems should have started you out on the road to appreciating what you do now, and how it could all be done much better. However, the task of listening is made a lot easier if a few simple rules are followed:

1. Make a deliberate and special effort to concentrate on the message itself. Don't allow yourself to get side-tracked by irrelevancies; just focus on the central theme of the message – what is it your partner *wants you to know*.
2. A common fault is to stop listening for a while so that you can get on with preparing your own reply to what you've heard. Give your whole attention to what is being said, and wait until your partner has finished. Don't worry about getting your views across – under the rules of the program you have the right to do *your* bit of thinking and to give an uninterrupted response when your turn comes around.
3. Similarly, don't start to analyze what you have heard before you have the complete picture. Distressed couples tend to jump far too readily to conclusions – just remember this, and don't make the mistake of trying to hurry the solution along.
4. When you are *listening* you're not doing the talking, so don't hassle your partner, rushing them along, trying to say it for them. Just listen patiently.
5. Be *interested* in what your partner has to say. Try to show this in your manner and expression: look at your partner and follow the rules of non-verbal communication set out earlier in this chapter.
6. Showing you are interested and giving your partner feedback about how you feel is helped by two kinds of action:

    (a) Whenever your partner does or says something that you like and enjoy, show this by smiling, giving verbal encouragement or by any other way that informs about your good feelings.

    (b) To give some indication of how you react to less good news is also permissible, but it must not be in an aggressive way. The correct way is to make the point and tell how it could be done better. For example, it is wrong to say:

       'How many times do I have to tell you . . .'
       'You must be out of your mind to . . .'
       'You're simply not interested in . . .'
       'Why can't you stop acting like . . .'

The correct and positive way of communicating would be:

'When you went out yesterday you left a lot of mess for me to clear up. I would have liked to have your help in getting that work done.'

In short, the correct way is to say what is wrong in a quite factual way and explain what change you would like, in the same manner.

7. In your attempts at communication there is an obligation to make sure you understand what your partner is saying. Few of us can *always* say things in the clearest possible way, and distressed couples have greater difficulty than most in putting across their ideas. Accordingly, you should seek clarification of what your partner has said, doing this in a measured and unemotional way.

There are many examples of where we are inclined to assume we know what is meant, but could quite easily get it wrong. If, for example, your partner says 'I wish you hadn't mentioned my visit to the doctor in front of the neighbors', it is quite clear what *was not* wanted, but not fully evident what *is needed* in the future. Does the statement mean that this particular visit should have been kept secret? Are all visits to the doctor to be regarded as private information? Does it mean that you are a bit of a blabbermouth and this is just another example of you talking too much? These and other interpretations may be made, so it is important, at a suitable time, to find out. The way to do so is to say:

'I wondered what you meant when you said . . .'
'I'm not entirely certain what you mean about . . .'
'What exactly do you have in mind when you say . . .'
and so on.

These questions must be put in a *positive* and a *calm* way, making sure that your partner sees that you are not trying to be difficult but, on the contrary, wanting to understand so that you can be more compliant. Such questions should be asked as many times as required, until you feel that you know just what your partner has in mind, remembering that the full meaning may not have been included if you have only heard the words themselves (remember non-verbal signals).

8. In your listening time it is a very good thing to avoid what may seem to your partner like studied disinterest. Showing that you *are* interested in what he or she has to say is helped by talking (ask questions) to your partner about themselves. In fact, this is just part of the old adage that a good conversationalist talks to you about yourself and a bad one talks to you about himself, but it is really a bit more than a conversational ploy in this case. What is required is that you make a series of questions or comments without digressing to your own point of view. There are, therefore, right and wrong ways of doing this:

Wrong:
'Are you upset?'
'very much so.'
'I got pretty upset myself the other day.'

This is a digression to talking about how *you* felt and doesn't explore why your partner feels upset right now.

Right:
'Are you upset?'
'Very much so.'
'Can we talk about it?'

This shows interest in your partner's feelings and you can go on to help him or her to let go and spell out what is causing the distress.

Wrong:
'Do you feel like making love?'
'No, not really.'
'Whenever I feel that way I try to think of . . .', etc.
Right:
'Do you feel like making love?'
'No, not really.'
'Shall I put on some of the music you like?'

The difference between these two ways of asking questions should now be obvious.

A few final aids to getting your own message across

In one way or another we are involved in a great deal of communication with our partners. Even when words are not in use, we can and do convey 'messages' by the way we act, the pose we adopt, or even our presence or absence from a room. As previous chapters indicated, it is the purpose of this book to tell you how to make changes in your behavior so that both you and your partner can improve your relationship. Many of these changes will be arranged through the kind of formal negotiations in which you both give and get. You both agree to make some change, and you trade the alterations you have made.

But much of our communication will take place outside these formal settings and, while some things that are going wrong need to be sorted out by sitting down to negotiate solutions to the problem, the rules of good communication also apply to everyday situations. So, be ready to apply the following points to aid the way you communicate with your partner.

1. Be concise. Good communication doesn't mean that a lengthy review of old issues and history is required. Keep your points precise and relevant; don't use 'talking' to hold your partner to ransom, claiming that he or she is obliged to hear you out in long rambling solo performances.
2. Eliminate any tendency to make confessions, or to complicate the problem under discussion. Baring your soul and making revelations is generally not helpful, so confine your talk to the here-and-now problem.
3. Don't try to mislead your partner, nor distort your message in an attempt to soften the blow. Brutal frankness isn't helpful, but you should aim at being direct and honest about the problem and the way you feel about it.
4. Direct self-expression is best achieved when you use 'I', showing that you accept full personal responsibility for what is being said. Avoid starting with:

    'Everybody would agree with me that . . .'
    'It's very obvious to other people that . . .'
    'They say we should . . .'
    'My mother thinks . . .'

It is *your* message and it reflects how *you* personally feel. You don't need 'them' – or your uncle – to support what you say; the use of others tends to be counterproductive.

5. Keep your partner involved. Communication is a two-way process and the purpose of 'talking' isn't to enable you to blow off steam or air your grievances – it is a problem-solving activity. Keeping your partner involved is helped by making your point, and then getting his or her reaction to it. Some simple examples of this are:

'I'd like to go for a walk . . . would you like to come along too?'
'I think we should spend more on education for the kids . . . do you think we can afford it?'
'I feel we ought to do a bit more socializing . . . how do you feel about inviting the neighbors for a drink?'

6. It goes without saying that you should choose the right moment to make some important act of communication.

Joe, anxious to get to grips with the problems he and Rosemary were having, tried to raise these issues pretty well as soon as he got home from work. Rosemary was usually at her busiest at this time, trying to get the meal cooked and the children ready for bed, and tended to react irritably at this time. To Joe this seemed like a rebuff and a sign of Rosemary's unwillingness to get down to dealing with their difficulties.

It is important to try to set aside time for those special occasions when you are going to discuss behavior changes. Don't try to hurry these along too quickly, as you will need to be in the right frame of mind to solve problems. Try to arrange a regular time and frequency for these discussions, but be ready to make some modification to your schedule without getting upset about it. Certainly, don't force the issue if your partner is in a bad mood, very tired, or is deeply involved in some other activity at the time when *you* are ready to talk.

But it is also important that such opportunities are not passed over and, if anything, talking time has priority over other things. You should be willing to sacrifice other pursuits in order to get your personal relationship in better repair.

SUMMARY OF THE BASIC RULES FOR GOOD COMMUNICATION

1. Choose the right words; avoid tendencies to insult, punish, threaten, and denigrate your partner.
2. Eliminate the negatives in your communication.
3. Be positive; don't say what you won't or can't do, say what you can and want to do.
4. Be open and honest, but also tactful. Don't hide your message, but do put it in a constructive and helpful way.
5. Talk as if you care. Be interested in your partner's feelings and needs. Try to think of her/him – be *empathic*.
6. Use your voice tone, facial expression, and bodily posture to show your *positive feelings*.
7. Don't use your talk sessions as an opportunity to nag, complain, bring up old resentments, or hog the conversation.
8. Listen to your partner – don't dwell on your reaction or what you will say; just focus on what your partner is saying.
9. When listening, encourage your partner's disclosures by asking questions.
10. When you are doing the talking be concise, relevant, positive, and clear. Begin with 'I' to show *you* accept responsibility for what you are saying.
11. Keep your partner involved by the 'Keep in touch' rule and use this to make sure you understand his/her viewpoint.
12. When talking has been difficult, try writing down the points you want to discuss.

CHAPTER 5

How to Handle Conflict and Anger

Sophie and Dean had both remarried late in life. Both had enjoyed excellent first marriages which had, sadly, ended with the death of their partners. Neither had even begun to think about taking another partner in life but had thought of themselves as a 'one-man woman' and a 'one-woman man'. They had settled down to the solitary existence that had become their lot, their children having grown up and left home.

So, each of them spent the next decade in this way until, in their early sixties, they were introduced by a friend. Dean was 'a real gentleman'; considerate, courteous, and just a little old-fashioned in his relationships with the opposite sex. He was, however, popular, good natured, and quite sociable. Sophie was 'a perfect lady', gentle, amiable, and generous-spirited. Furthermore, both Sophie and Dean were good-looking and youthful in appearance, their middle-class background provided much in common for them, and their many friends on both sides thought of their decision to marry as wonderful. Indeed, everyone they knew saw them as an ideal couple who would bring great happiness to each other.

To the utter astonishment of all their friends, Sophie and Dean quarreled bitterly from the very start of their marriage. There was simply no issue on which they saw eye-to-eye, and it was clear that they had reached the stage where the part of the toothpaste tube that was squeezed, or the type of breakfast cereal preferred, had become battlegrounds. Although Sophie's friends could still see in her all the qualities that made her so personable, and although those who knew Dean well still knew him as a gentleman, in their private lives the two of them fought like cat and dog.

They separated within a few months of marrying, and no attempt to reconcile their differences was successful; both were utterly convinced that they had made a tragic error which needed to be put right as soon as possible. So far as one could tell, in the brief time spent in trying to deal with this problem, they had brought to their marriage a curious idealism – a kind of impossible dream that consisted, very substantially, of treasured memories of their dead partners. Both, it seems, measured up the new partner with the idealized recollections of their old relationship and found a mismatch. It may well have been, too, that they had both been rather unchanging people, making little modification to their personal lifestyles over the years and, in their ten years of living alone, they had become firmly entrenched in their own ways. Changes, for both of them, were quite unthinkable.

Zoe and Frank, on the other hand, have been married for just four years, for the first two of which they seemed to have got along quite well. However, two years ago a couple of significant changes occurred in their lives, Zoe having their first child and Frank's mother coming to live with them. From that time their relationship deteriorated significantly, and now they find it hard to exchange a friendly word with each other. At interview they avoid eye contact, they tend to talk about each other through the interviewer rather than addressing remarks directly to one another, while accusations and counter-accusations are thick in the air. Their problems are now much wider than how Zoe is coping with the baby or how to deal with Frank's demanding mother. In the way all too familiar in collapsing relationships, they find cause to quarrel about anything and everything.

For Zoe and Frank there is a kind of understanding that they have let matters get out of focus and, more important, despite their arguments, there is still a measure of affection – or at least an awareness that they *did* love and *could* still love each other. They want to stay together and they want to have help to achieve this. Each acknowledges that the other has burdens to bear; Frank recognizes that Zoe can't do quite what she used to do for him because of the baby, while Zoe appreciates that Frank is caught between wanting to help his mother and feeling put out by her always being around. They see some of their problems clearly enough, but seem to have no good way of dealing with them, and their conflict has escalated and spread to all areas of their lives together.

At least, rather than take the view that their marriage is a sinking ship to be abandoned, they acknowledge that there are real problems and they are willing to try to save the relationship.

Angry exchanges are commonplace; conflict is part and parcel of sharing our lives with others, and it would be quite remarkable if we found ourselves in relationships where there were no disagreements or differences. Yet, there are two distinguishing features about the conflict to be observed in the distressed couple:

1. The frequency and intensity of rows is much greater than in relationships that are healthy.
2. There are no well-developed ways of de-escalating conflicts.

In short, we find once again that it is not that distressed couples have unusual problems, but that these problems assume proportions out of keeping with their true seriousness, and the couple have no ready means of resolving them. So, two basic considerations follow from this: to keep the problems in perspective and to learn how to deal with angry feelings.

ANGER IS DESTRUCTIVE

It is often said by the well-adjusted couple that there is nothing quite like a good fight so that you can get something out of your system and, in any case, it is great to make up afterwards! Perhaps, for some people, the occasional row does 'clear the air' and helps the couple to avoid becoming too complacent but, in general, we are forced to conclude that anger is a destructive influence rather than a useful safety valve. Not infrequently things are said or done in anger that leave a lasting influence long after the strong emotions have cooled. The things said or done in anger can often contain a grain of truth – at least as perceived by the recipient – and can put a barrier between the couple that need not have been there.

Yet, of course, we are all vulnerable to the experience

KEEF

It's great to make up afterwards

strong negative feelings. We all feel that, at times, our rights are being ignored, some injustice has been done, we have suffered a blow to our feelings and aspirations, or have failed to get a fair hearing from others. Maybe, feeling upset about something that happened outside our relationship, we transfer the hostility to our partner and, in countless other ways, become a victim of anger.

In fact it is much easier for us to direct our frustration and annoyance toward our partner and to treat them with a discourtesy and offensiveness we wouldn't dream of using with strangers. We feel secure in doing so, letting rip safe in the knowledge that there are ties in our relationship that can't easily be broken. Anyhow, we may say, our partners are going to be around to make up again, unlike our more distant contacts who may forever avoid us following a 'bust up'. There are some who take advantage of this closeness by *expecting* to be allowed to erupt into violent emotion on little provocation, but want this to be overlooked each time it happens. They feel that their partners should 'know by now what I'm like, and that it soon blows over for me.' This is often a dangerous indulgence and we have no fundamental right to expect our frequent outbursts to be forgiven simply because we are 'like that'; rather, we have a responsibility *not* to be 'like that', and it is our obligation to learn an alternative way of behaving.

Some conflicts surface and blaze only briefly, quickly fizzling out because one partner is always ready to back off. This encourages the 'winner' to use the same ploy again and again, since the distate for argument is strong in the other person. Indeed, some boast that there is never a cross word in the relationship, failing to recognize that they have actively inhibited any show of similar feelings in their partners.

A more serious aspect of those relationships where overt challenges are not made, is that **the problems remain unsolved** and the 'submissive' partner may resort to means other than anger of expressing his or her feelings. Sometimes it is this partner who finally 'wins', because the indirect way of achieving victory – the tactic of 'being difficult' – is not open to direct challenge. Such warfare is the hallmark of the failing relationship.

Despite their best endeavors to avoid such difficulties, the troubled couple will tend to find themselves in conflict. All their efforts to reduce this by making sound contracts, establishing well-negotiated behavior changes, and by achieving good communication, may not be entirely successful in heading off rows. In such cases, clashes can occur of a damaging and sustained type and what has been learned so far does not protect them from losing what they had earlier gained. De-escalating conflict is a desirable aim in its own right and the rules can be useful even in marriages marked by primarily good relationships, as well as in those in urgent need of repair.

PLAIN ANGER IS WRONG

When we become angry there is an accompanying need for instant and full recompense for perceived injury. We demand restitution and insist on remorse and capitulation from the 'offending' person. Anger narrows down our viewpoint so that we see only our own side of the story, and we can convince ourselves that we – and only we – have right on our side. For these reasons anger is a dangerous state in relationships, and the control of this feeling is of great importance.

ANGER IS COUNTER-PRODUCTIVE

When we are in discussions with our partners, arranging changes or in other ways reflecting our emotions and attitudes, it is quite appropriate to indicate our strength of feeling. It is, indeed, important to let one's partner know of upset or distress caused by one thing or another, but belligerent, assaultative behavior, simply getting incoherently angry with our partner, blinds us to whatever alternative views can be taken. Furthermore, and just as significant, is that anger begets anger; that is, this emotion tends to **produce the same behavior** in those against whom it is directed. It is a common observation that attacks made by one partner, perhaps about some quite trivial matter, produce angry retorts and soon the couple are caught up in escalating conflict, both being carried away on a tide of emotion. Neither seems able to control the release of anger, or even want to put a stop to the matter. Sometimes, even mild and otherwise easy-going individuals, who 'wouldn't hurt a fly', commit absurd and unjustifiable physical attacks on their partner, engage in self-injurious behavior, or simply rush out into the night in uncontrollable fury.

John and Vera were victims of such escalating emotions. They usually managed to confine their anger to shouting abuse, leaving each other sickened, confused, and dismayed and with the terrified children coming downstairs to plead with them to stop. But on this occasion John slammed out of the house, got into his car, and drove recklessly into the night, his blind rage only subsiding when he smashed into a tree. The accident shook him greatly, but he could see how lucky he was that he had not killed some innocent person by his recklessness. He felt overwhelmed by misery, too, in seeing how his inability to deal with his marriage problems led him into such dangerous reactions.

AIM TO SOLVE PROBLEMS

It has already been said that each partner in the failing marriage believes that he or she is right. If only the other person could behave well, have the right approach, be a little more like this or that, then everything would be alright. In short, the relationship problems are the other person's fault. It follows from this, of course, that conflicts are all about the shortcomings of the partner; if one is at fault at all, then it is only that one is giving tit for tat. 'Why', the infuriated partners will each declare, 'should I allow my wife/husband just to walk all over me; anyone who knew what he/she really is like would be bound to agree with me,' and so on. Conflicts, then, are about winning, about getting one's own back, about retaliation, about bringing one's partner to book and about punishing him/her for wrongdoing. Unfortunately, conflicts have very little to do with solving problems.

If they are to get the problem under control, the couple must first appreciate that winning arguments by inflicting damage or hurt on their 'opponent' doesn't help. A war of attrition, in which you both slug it out to the bitter end, not only debilitates everyone but offers no cure for the ailment. The aim must be to **solve your problem**.

Conflict is inevitable in human relationships, and the resolution of conflict should be a gain *for both sides* arising out of a mutually agreed solution to any issue. This brings us back, once again to managing agreed changes to our own and our partner's behavior.

BREAKING DOWN THE PROBLEM

It is really very surprising to find that bitter feelings and open warfare have been inspired by events that are often easy to explain and not difficult to deal with.

Pat and Bill had a number of conflicts in their marriage, but one of Pat's most strongly felt views was about Bill's going out drinking several times each week – leaving her to cope 'with everything.' Especially annoying was Bill's tendency to ring her if he had got too drunk to say he would be staying overnight with one of his drinking buddies. Essentially, Pat's complaints boiled down to:

(a) Bill spends too many evenings away from home.
(b) Pat feels he ought to help out more with the chores at home.
(c) Pat disapproves of Bill becoming paralytically drunk and staying away overnight.

It was quite easy for Bill and Pat to come to an agreement which involved:

(a) Cutting down Bill's drinking nights by half.

(b) Bill helping with specific evening chores – although, as it happened, there were relatively few of them. Primarily it was Pat's pique at being left alone that was the real complaint, rather than that she had too much to do.

(c) Bill agreeing to cut his drinking to avoid getting very drunk, and always coming home even if he had to get a taxi.

The rows about this issue, which had been commonplace, disappeared. Pat felt that she had got a reasonable deal and Bill felt it was no great hardship to make the changes he had undertaken. Indeed, he became interested in carpentry – which he had given up some years before – and spent more time in this activity, which pleased Pat too.

STICK TO THE ISSUE

Conflict between partners invariably presents an opportunity for opening old wounds and re-fighting old battles. Escalation of both scale and intensity of conflict is guaranteed when this happens. There is also a golden opportunity for resorting to the generalizations and assertions mentioned earlier in this book, such as 'you don't love me', 'you're utterly selfish', or charges of 'weakness, 'irresponsibility', 'jealousy', 'never listening', and so on. So, the arguments roll along familiar tracks to well-known destinations of shouting, character-assassination, and other forms of abuse.

People in conflict must observe the rule of sticking to the issue at hand, whatever that happens to be. Matters irrelevant and unconnected are not to be discussed so that, like Bill and Pat, the nature of **this** problem can be identified and a solution to **this** problem can be agreed.

If George has arrived home much later than he said, Sybil may raise the roof, calling him 'absolutely uncaring' and 'irresponsible.' When they can talk about this later, and when George has stopped being quite so defensive about being late, the couple may be able to re-label the problem and decide that George seems to have difficulty in leaving work before other people and this happens because:

(a) He is too inclined to be helpful to his colleagues by spending time talking to them about their problems after work.

(b) He is worried about redundancy and doesn't want his boss to identify him as someone not pulling his weight.
(c) He takes a lot of pride in his work and wants to do a good job, so once he gets involved in something he wants to finish the work before he leaves.

Once George has honestly given an account of what he is doing and why he is doing it, he and Sybil can get around to deciding what action to take. Maybe George can learn not to worry so much about being among the first people to leave the factory, or maybe he can re-schedule his helpful talks with his friends, perhaps inviting them around one evening with their wives. It isn't possible to do much about 'not caring' or being 'absolutely irresponsible', but there is a chance of doing something about the *real* causes of George's late homecoming.

The answer is found in describing the actual behavior that occurred and why it happened. Generalizations and accusations don't help us to do that; only sticking to the issue can focus our minds on problem solving.

SETTING THE SCENE

Negative emotions like anger and fear, although very powerful, tend to decrease quite rapidly over time. These emotions blaze strongly and, during this phase, we may do and say things that will have lasting consequences. Marriage counselors are frequently employed in trying to explain that, when in a state of extreme upset, we are all given to the kind of distortions that are much better forgotten. But, for the victim of such episodes, the memory fades far less quickly than the anger that triggered it. Sometimes, too, we find the 'victim' is happy to make what was said or done in anger a collector's item – a ghost to be raised again and again, proof positive of the 'true' feelings and intentions of the perpetrator.

Where anger did prompt stupid words or actions (and it rarely fails to do so), these must be 'forgotten' in the interests of getting down to solving real problems. It is obviously much better to avoid the ventilation of anger altogether, if this can be managed. Remember, it is not wrong to *feel* anger or to *be* angry: it *is* wrong to allow this emotion to get *out of control*. So, recognizing that the feeling is only intense for a brief period of time, try the following rules to see if you can *gain control* over such emotion. If you do, then you are in a much better position to solve your problem which, after all, is the really important objective, *not* the damage you can inflict in two minutes of blazing fury.

1. Do not try to reason things through when anger is at its height. You will almost certainly fail because reasonableness just isn't likely at that time. If you are on the receiving end of anger, try to remain quiet and don't attempt to interrupt your partner or challenge him/her until the main wave of anger has passed.
2. If you are the angry partner, try a little 'paradoxical intention' – that is, set out to be or do something in a deliberate way – and find it more difficult to make a good job of it! This is a bit like making a conscious effort to walk downstairs – as soon as you try to get away from the well-rehearsed automatic way, you stumble and falter. Or, to give another example, when you try *not* to think of an elephant it becomes pretty well impossible to keep elephants out of your mind. In short, you tell your partner that you are going to get angry, that you may start to shout and rage, and so on, and the effect is often a rather diluted rage reaction.
3. A good third rule is to change the scene from where the angry explosion is to (or would) take place, to another where anger is going to be diminished. Don't stand in the kitchen or hall to let rip, go into the lounge, sit down, make a cup of coffee, and put yourself in a situation where anger will be contained. Any small delay will be helpful in allowing the sharp edge of anger to become blunted, and it is certainly more difficult to give anger full rein when sitting comfortably, drinking coffee.

DISTRACT YOUR ANGER

To an extent, 'changing the scene' as described above could be said to be a distraction imposed by altering your external environment. However, a good deal of control can be gained by the angry person by creating *internal* distractions. A good example of this is the use of what is known as 'thought stopping' with individuals who suffer from persistent worrying thoughts. Using this technique, the individual learns to inhibit the unwanted thought by using some signal, such as the word 'stop'. We can also make use of what is known as 'attention switching', in which we develop the ability to turn our attention from one thing to another, at will.

A difficulty with these techniques is that they tend to require expert advice and guidance before they can be used effectively. Furthermore, as will be appreciated, the individual beset by anxious and worrying ideas actually *wants* to be rid of such thoughts, while the angry person often seems to enjoy the explosive release of his or her emotion. Nevertheless, we can make use of some aspects of the techniques referred to, recognizing that anger seems to feed on its own presence, and the following rules will help in gaining control:

1. First, remember that we *can* exercise control; we don't *have* to become uncontrollably angry and we *choose* to allow this to happen.
2. Be vigilant about anger. This emotion can be and usually is anticipated, we allow it to build up until it reaches an explosive level. It is during the early stages of 'build'up' that we have the best chance of exercising control, so it is here that we must start to take charge. Once our anger has reached its highest point there is less chance of doing anything about it.
3. When anger is building up (e.g. waiting for someone to arrive who is going to be very late), rather than allow yourself to feed these feelings with provocative ideas such as 'she doesn't care . . .', 'he's treating me with contempt', and so on, **deliberately distract yourself**. This is not easy to do; we need to *want to do it* and we need to make *an effort to do it*. Turn your mind to thoughts about any pleasant (or neutral) topic, such as the new decorative scheme for the sitting room, the job in the garden you are planning for the weekend, or the holiday you enjoyed so much last year. Try to fix these ideas in your mind, see yourself engaged in these activities in your mind's eye.

In short, the way to blunt angry thoughts is to catch them at their weakest and deliberately to distract ourselves from them. When the time comes for problem-solving, for telling your partner about your feelings and getting the matter in some perspective, you will be much better prepared. At this stage the rules that need to be observed can be set out separately for the angry and the offending partner.

FOR THE ANGRY PARTNER

BE READY TO TALK

1. An important first step is to show clearly that you are ready to get down to solving the problem through discussion. Many conflicts rumble on, unresolved, until the next conflict arises and there is little room for peaceful relationships. It can be hard for the individual who feels himself or herself to be the victim of out-rageous treatment to let the other person off the hook but, by continuing an unrelenting warfare, the chance for reaching a solution to the problem is wasted.

Anger should be about letting the other person know how strongly you feel, its purpose being to discourage further hurtful behavior by the other person. But, since anger is often exagger-ated, misguided, and protracted, it usually fails to achieve its objectives. So, it is most important to show a willingness to deal with the issue through discussion.

STATE THE PROBLEM CLEARLY

2. The discussions need to begin with a clear and unambiguous statement of the problem. Don't be tempted to raise old issues but focus your partner's attention upon what it is **here and now** that has upset you so much.

DON'T RAISE THE TEMPERATURE

3. Talking about the problem in this way sometimes leads to a surge of stronger feelings and you may be tempted to allow negative attitudes of a general kind to surface in your mind, such as 'I'm not going to let him get away with it this time', or 'I'll really teach her a lesson she'll never forget . . .' These ideas offer very temporary relief to the angry individual, and the price one pays for entertaining them is a very heavy one. Forget such notions, try to keep to the issue and don't be seduced by ideas of giving your partner a bad time.

DON'T SET OUT TO WIN

4. Get rid of any idea that your discussion is an argument in which there will be a winner and a loser and that you, feeling very

upset, are going to win this one anyway. **There are no winners in such conflicts, only losers**. The people who gain from proper discussion and problem-solving are you and your partner. Just consider the well-publicized angry displays of tennis players or footballers, and ask yourself how many times such people actually win the argument (even if they win the match), and how contemptible they seem to the detached observer. Make sure you don't set out to win in this ineffectual and self-destructive way.

TRY WRITING YOUR MESSAGE

5. If you find it very difficult to get your anger under control and feel your emotions will spill over in rage, tears, or in some other way, try to write down, in a letter to your partner, just what is bothering you. Again, keep to the issue and don't be tempted to bring in all kinds of old arguments and irrelevances. You may find that you can get your thoughts together much better by writing them down than by talking and, later, when your partner has had a chance to read your letter, then you can come together for your discussion about solving the problem.

TELL YOUR PARTNER WHAT WOULD HELP

6. When you have told your partner about what it is that has made you so upset and got his or her reaction to it, then go on to say precisely what it is that would help. Some problems obviously can't be 'put right' in the sense that one can't really restore the broken vase to its original state, or put back the clock so that the affair didn't take place. Problem solving must focus on the *future*, not the past, so the discussion doesn't dwell on shortcomings and recriminations but on how to build a better relationship and reduce the possibility of hurt all over again. To do this you will need to cut out any threats and exaggerated demands; just confine your talk to indicating, as clearly as you can, what *would* have been right for your partner to do, and what he or she can do now and in the future to solve the problem.

START WITH A POSITIVE

7. When you are angry and feel hurt it is hard to be positive with your partner. However, your aim is to introduce changes into his

Say precisely what it is that would help

or her behavior. The way you put your points – either in a negative or a positive way – will affect the reaction you receive, the sincerity of your partner, and his or her cooperation in dealing with the issue. Getting your partner *on your side* in appreciating how you feel, understanding why you feel this way, and how you can both deal with it, is your main objective. So try to put your points in the positive ways outlined in the previous chapter on communication (Chapter 4).

John had put off, for the second time that week, his promise to take Crispin to practice swimming for the school water sports gala. Crispin was angry, sulky and went upstairs, kicking the stair-rails, when it became clear that his father had agreed to get the firm's accounts ready for a meeting tomorrow and would need all the time he could get that evening. Susan was livid. To her this was typical of her husband's casualness about promises made, both to her and the kids, and this was simply the last straw. Always, she felt, she had to make alterations to her own plans to fit in with John's changes of mind and, to her, this new incident revealed just how he took them all for granted, ignoring their feelings, ambitions, and needs. Total selfishness, that's what it was.

Susan didn't seriously try to put the problem into perspective. She could have discovered that John was under enormous strain at work at the time and was only just managing to hang on, so to speak. She could have got to know that John felt he was 'keeping going' in this way for the sake of the family, not to spite or disregard them. She could have found that John would have loved to go along to the pool with Crispin and, indeed, took pride, pleasure, and kudos from Crispin's swimming prowess. But she didn't manage to look at any of these things: she focussed on the anger welling up inside her and just let rip that evening.

Better by far would have been an attempt to discuss with John her feelings and thoughts about what had happened. She should not have started such a discussion with an accusation, but with a positive and 'understanding' remark, such as 'I know you're going through a bad patch at the moment' or 'You seem to have a lot on your plate these days', and then move on to her specific complaint. Doing this she not only indicates that she is aware things aren't just to be reduced to simply 'I'm right and you are wrong', but also shows a willingness to consider different points of view. Just as important, she allows John to develop a mental approach that gets him to focus on the problem without the need to become too defensive or react in a belligerent way. So, the rule here is to start your discussion with a positive remark rather than rushing into an aggressive tirade.

DON'T HIDE YOUR ANGER

8. Anger is justifiable. Not, of course, uncontrolled aggression and wild accusation, but an understandable show of feeling about something you see as wrong and unacceptable. It is not necessary to disguise your frustration and annoyance and, in-deed, it is useful to show this emotion to your partner. You can begin by saying 'I know I really lost my temper when you . . .', or 'I simply flew into a blind rage when . . .' You concede your emotion and, in doing so, show how strongly you feel and your

readiness to put the feeling into proper perspective. You are not apologizing for being angry or excusing your emotion; you are simply giving an account of your feelings and the particular behavior of your partner that brought them into being. You don't have to feel guilty about these feelings, but *it is your responsibility to maintain control*, to be fair in your statements, and to seek solutions to problems.

An understandable show of feelings

LISTEN TO YOUR PARTNER

9. In the example given above, Susan didn't even want to listen to John. Once she had let her anger out in a torrent of abuse and personal hurt, she experienced enough guilt to prevent her telling John that she had overstated the case. So, she continued to defend her anger as entirely justifiable and in no way regretted. This effectively prevented the couple arriving at an understanding of the problem and a solution to it.

Getting changes to behavior involves listening to your partner as Chapter 4 described and, in most cases, anger has to be cooled when the other side of a problem is looked at. But often we don't feel inclined to listen when we are angry and the more upset we get, the narrower our viewpoint. Yet a conscious effort to listen is essential to resolving conflict. As Susan could have discovered, the things John had to say about his lapse made his behavior both more understandable and excusable – and could even have led to Susan offering more help to *him*. Certainly, Susan's global charges of selfishness were wrong and it would have been more appropriate for them to discuss other topics, such as:

1. John's over-conscientiousness.
2. His over eagerness to be the company's 'willing horse'.
3. How Susan can help him get the accounts ready if he does take Crispin to the pool
4. John's tendency to over value work as the means of helping the family, when such attitudes stop him doing precisely that.

And so on.

   Listening to your partner helps you to examine the problem from a different standpoint and, as you will see from the above, it is possible to work on and rectify a problem that you *can* pin down more precisely. It is obvious that Susan's generalizations about John being 'uncaring' and 'taking them all for granted' don't help. Not only are they untrue but they offer no possibility for John to make any changes that are needed.

FOR THE 'OFFENDING' PARTNER

The term 'offending' is used here simply to indicate the person against whom anger is directed. It will be clear from what has been said that it is not always the case that the anger is justified, even though the angry partner feels this way.

   Chris felt utterly devastated when Beverley told him she was thinking of leaving. He had begun to suspect that something was wrong about two months earlier, when she had roughly rejected his reaching out for her in bed. He'd hoped this was just a bad mood but, as the weeks passed, it became evident that something more fundamental was wrong. At last, after nights of worried interrogation by Chris, Beverley told him that she was interested in someone else and then, later, that she planned to leave him.

Chris was stunned and incredulous. He felt their relationship had been happy, and couldn't understand how Beverley could be ready to leave him and the children to live with a man he thought of as a total stranger. He also got angry and depressed, couldn't sleep, lost weight, couldn't cope with his job, and felt totally helpless. Sometimes he wanted to leave the marriage, to throw Beverley out (she had decided to conduct her affair from her home), and his hatred for her would erupt into rages that scared the children. But, at other times, he felt desolated by what had happened and pleaded with Beverley to give up her relationship. He felt he had made a fool of himself by going around to the 'other man', begging him in a publicly humiliating way to leave his wife alone and, at times, he plotted fearful revenge. Constantly, Chris was subject to tumultuous feelings that left him sick and afraid and, on occasions, he would actually vomit as a result of the strain he was under. Indeed, he felt at times that he would go mad with the tension.

At this stage Chris felt that it was all the fault of his wife. His rage was directed toward her, his feeling of loathing was 'understandable', and the threat to the children was entirely of her making. In no way could Chris see that he might have had something to do with Beverley's behavior, and the mere suggestion that the problem might have been other than one-sided was an insult to his intelligence. Yet, the more closely we examined their lives together before the affair, the clearer it became that all had not been well. For Chris, ahead lay the uphill struggle to recognize that, if his relationship was to be given a new chance, he would have to make changes and, for Beverley, the realization would be needed that her way of solving the problem was unfair and misguided.

For Beverley, too, there is the need to deal effectively with the storms that now rage in her relationship with Chris and, if she wants to stay together, then she must begin by renouncing the affair. Only when she has done this can she turn her attention to dealing with Chris's anger with certain rules in mind.

DON'T QUIT THE SITUATION

1. There is a great temptation in all of us to leave when anger is

being directed against us. Part of us, perhaps, wants to hit back, to damage the person treating us in this way, but part of us simply wants to quit. Storming out, rushing upstairs and slamming the door, and other ways of opting out give a temporary relief, but this doesn't solve problems. If you want to make a better relationship it is essential that you talk with your partner and, even if a cooling-off period is agreed, you must get back to discussing the issues.

Don't quit the situation

KEEP CALM AND LISTEN QUIETLY

2. During the period of intense anger expressed by your partner, remain quiet and don't interrupt the outpouring of rage. Trying

to get across your own views at this stage will be pretty well impossible; raging right back only escalates the conflict, and interruptions simply inflame your partner more. You must be patient and wait for the opportunity to involve your partner in a discussion about the problem. If you can, arrange this in another room, sitting down, close to your partner, with eye contact and following all the other rules for *good listening*.

GET CLOSE

3. During the intense period of anger, too, you should try to get physically close to your partner and show by your face and manner that you are concerned about what is happening. If possible, try to hold hands or put your arm around your partner; this is not always possible but does have great value if it can be managed.

DON'T HURRY THINGS ALONG

4. Don't try to get to the problem-solving stage too quickly and be overeager to agree that you were wrong and won't ever do it again. Instead, try to show *real* concern about what has gone wrong, using appropriate words to convey this; for example, 'I know you are very angry and upset and I really do want to help put things right again.' You must try patiently to hear out your partner and not try to brush aside his or her description of what is wrong.

Pauline complains that, frequently, Colin is very ready to say 'sorry' and cuts into her account of what has happened; in fact, she says, he quite often doesn't know what he is apologizing for, and she feels frustrated and annoyed by this.

BE READY TO ADMIT ERROR

5. If you can clearly see that you are at fault and have made a mistake that causes your partner to feel angry, be ready to admit this is so. Accept full responsibility for what has happened and don't attempt to bluster or make excuses. However, admitting you were wrong is not very much use unless it is accompanied by a resolve and real effort to do better and to make the necessary changes to your behavior.

HELP YOUR PARTNER

6. Help your partner to make his or her points in a constructive way. Ask questions that will clarify not only how you should have acted on this matter, but how he or she would feel about other similar issues. This will help your partner to appreciate your genuine concern about things and will aid you in getting a fuller understanding of what your partner expects. Try to identify exactly what steps you should take on some future occasion, and what signs to look out for.

DON'T MAKE COUNTER-ACCUSATIONS

7. Don't get involved in counter-accusations or cross-complaining. It is all too easy to do this, even in a mild way; for example, 'Well, if you hadn't . . .', or 'You often make a mess of . . .' It may be that there *are* things you would like to take up with your partner, but the resolution of *this* conflict is the priority right now, and your own complaint is irrelevant to deciding what may be done about the immediate problem.

REWARD EFFORT

8. Reward is an important way of firming up the solution to conflict. When you have been successful in getting a new under-standing and have agreed the changes that you will try to make in future, give your partner some real recognition of this. It may be just kind words, or it can be some material token that this issue is ended, but give or do something that marks the change. You are not saying that there will never be another argument or that you will never make another mistake – that would be unrealistic – but you are saying I *am* trying and I am doing my best to help our relationship along.

FOR BOTH PARTNERS

It is difficult for those whose relationship problems are few, to grasp the severity of stress which conflict can bring. Perpetual rows, the constant and unrelenting tension that both partners suffer, the harrowing effect on small children kept awake by outbreaks of unexplained rage in their parents are matters that, fortunately, are known to only some. Simply reducing conflict, whether or not that leads to a continuing relationship, is desirable in its own right, but securing a closer and improved contact with one's partner makes the effort supremely worthwhile.

A few general rules, to add to the list of specifics just given, will help you to achieve this objective.

CONSTRUCT A LIST OF COMMON GRIPES

First, it is a good idea to make a list of 'gripes' so that both partners can become aware of, and, avoid, behavior that is known to cause or contribute to anger. Such a list would not contain every source of conflict that *can* arise, but it Daniel knows that lateness home is a constant cause of acrimony, then he can keep a close eye on his time-keeping. If Stephanie bears in mind how she tends to appear rejecting when her husband wants to make love, then she could make a good contribution to conflict reduction. Both will be able to identify a number of particular and frequently occurring irritants which they should discuss with each other and do something to avoid. Of course, the list *must be specific* and not consist of vague generalizations such as 'be kinder', 'be more caring', and so on.

GREAT OAKS FROM LITTLE ACORNS

A second basic rule is to become more aware of the kind of thing that leads to conflict. It is useful to have the list referred to above, but it will be evident to many couples, when they come to consider the matter, that conflicts tend to grow, sometimes from quite small beginnings. By looking back at what has happened in the past, the couple can make themselves more aware of the remote and often petty beginnings to later bitter exchanges. Perhaps it began with Duncan leaving his dripping raincoat over the hall chair, or with Mandy forgetting to buy the razor blades Bill has especially asked her to get. Seeing the small beginnings reminds the couple of the triviality of these roots and that dealing with the small things can help to prevent a major conflagration later.

SECURE A TRUCE

A major confrontation is not usually settled easily, even when both partners have done their very best to implement the rules given. The feelings of hurt can go very deep and time may be needed for a full adjustment to be made, or anger may continue in a subdued form for some time to come and refuse to disappear. When this happens, recognize that not everything can be settled by one or two discussions and that the issue may need to be looked at again and again until it is resolved. What would be wrong is that, over the period of time in question, hostilities are continued. Rather, the couple should agree a truce which, while having limitations, would mean that there is deliberate avoidance of words or actions that would be sure to inflame matters. This may not be easy to do, but if the problem is to be resolved in an effective way, then this is the best means of achieving that end. It is not an impossible task, simply a hard one, and it is in our own interests that the effort is made.

To guide your attempts to deal with conflict, each partner should put a check mark, as appropriate, against the following statements:

I would like my partner to:

	He	She
1. Put forward more suggestions and a reasoned case about the problems.	....	....
2. Be more willing to cool things so that we can quickly get down to solving the problem.	....	....
3. Make reconciliation easier by such things as speaking kindly, touching gently, etc.	....	....
4. Be less willing to go on being cold, rejecting, and silent for long periods.	....	....
5. Be less ready to try and coerce me into giving in.	....	....
6. Show more willingness to accept a share of the blame.	....	....

At least this checklist will show you how your partner sees matters at the moment. It doesn't mean you are right and he (she) is wrong and, in any case, you may find that each of you will be checking the same item! If both of you *really do* want the kind of things you have checked in the list, you should start thinking of the changes to be made in your own behavior rather than in your partner's. If you are managing to live up to each of the points in a positive way, then the solution to conflict cannot be far off.

DON'T GET PERSONAL

Finally, don't personalize the conflict that needs to be solved by discussion. The agreement isn't helped along by 'You must be mad to think . . .', 'Your contempt for me has always been shown in . . .', 'This callousness of yours . . .', and so on. Stick to the issue itself so far as you possibly can, leaving out the personal construction you are tempted to put upon it.

SUMMARY OF THE POINTS IN THIS CHAPTER

1. Anger is a destructive force. It gets in the way of solving problems effectively and has long-term damaging influences on relationships.
2. Feeling angry is understandable and natural, but we must *control* anger, not allow it free rein.
3. Set aside time to discuss the reasons for anger – don't expect to settle the issue there and then in a show of rage.
4. In discussions stick to the issue. Don't allow your anger to spill over into old complaints and past grievances.
5. Try paradoxical intention – tell your partner you are going to be angry.
6. Change the scene – get away from the place where anger was shown – sit down and keep close to your partner.
7. Deliberately keep negative thoughts out of mind during the period before the discussion of the issue – don't brood and rehearse the problem.
8. Show readiness to discuss and don't set out to win the argument – just aim at clarifying your view and solving the problem.
9. Get your thoughts and feelings down on paper, sticking to the issue and not being sidetracked by irrelevances.
10. Make clear to your partner how he or she can help to reduce the conflict between you.

11. Start your exchanges of ideas with a deliberate positive – say an understanding thing before telling your partner of the cause of your anger.

12. Listent to your angry partner, don't argue back. Seek clarification of precisely what is wrong. Don't quit the situation.

13. Keep calm and don't make counter-accusations to your angry partner.

14. Be ready to admit mistakes but don't hurry things to a hasty conclusion before you find our exactly what is wrong.

15. Try to construct a list of common problems that lead to argument. Look at this list and try to do something about them – don't let the same old issue keep catching you by surprise.

16. Don't expect to solve all problems in one discussion session. Be ready to 'call a truce' – and keep it – during the time you are trying to get a major problem resolved.

CHAPTER 6

How to Make Decisions

Elsie complains that Eric leaves everything to her. She makes the point in an injured tone but, at the same time, seems to take a kind of pride in the burdens she claims she is forced to bear. Eric readily admits that Elsie is far more competent than he to manage the payment of bills, social arrangements, buying birthday presents, and so on, and isn't at all put out by Elsie taking over in these matters. In fact, Eric has abandoned decision making almost completely, leaving Elsie in sole charge. She, in her turn, has been highly critical of Eric's shortcomings over the years and has been inclined to regard him as pretty ineffectual about getting things done.

Elsie is a dominant personality while Eric is quite the opposite. From her point of view it is Eric's basic incompetence that has landed her in the position of having to make all the decisions while, from his, it is a case of settling for a quiet life.

The aim in helping this couple to come to terms with decision-making is to find an appropriate balance which will allow Elsie to feel that Eric is pulling his weight and enable him to exercise whatever competence he feels he might have. There are, of course, at least two other possibilities that could be considered.

DON'T AIM TO CUT IT DOWN THE MIDDLE

1. To reach a theoretical 'ideal' solution, in the sense that a 50/50 split could be arranged, with equal responsibilities for both

partners. The problem here is that neither Elsie nor Eric want this form of 'democracy' and would be unhappy if it were imposed on them.

DON'T AIM AT PERSONALITY CHANGE

2. To see the problem as one requiring therapy to reduce an excess of dominance in Elsie and a lack of assertiveness in Eric. This, too, is not a particularly useful solution (although based on the reality of their situation), since making these changes would be very difficult and could provoke further major problems for two people in advanced middle age.

THE MUTUAL AGREEMENT

Making changes is rarely about achieving theoretically ideal solutions, making couples conform to one's own or to a 'generally accepted' standard. To do so would be a grave disservice to the special circumstances and unique personality mix found in any partnership. Making changes is all about arriving at a mutually agreeable solution to a problem perceived by one or both partners to the relationship.

Glynis and Harold have a special problem in decision-making. They are rivals, both seeing anything to be decided upon only in their own personal light, each wanting the decision to be made in that way. They get into fights about most issues, from the kind of food they eat to what time to go to bed, each striving to gain authority.

For other couples the problem is different again, with both partners wanting to shed responsibility for decisions, sometimes because they want to avoid blame and sometimes because it is a convenient way of attaching blame to others. Dale and Millicent, for example, are always passing the buck, each refusing to accept responsibility for things that go wrong and claiming that the other should have taken care of it. Where money is concerned, Dale is always yelling at Millicent about what he sees as her overspending, while she tells him that it's his job to be budgethol-der and to let her know if he doesn't want to eat or the kids to wear shoes. They have no plan at all for how they spend their money, they have no budget, and they fail to make any checks upon where it is all going. There is, in short, no decision making for Dale and Millicent in this or any other area of their life together.

DOING WHAT COMES NATURALLY

For the most part we allow the decision-making in our relationships to grow out of tradition, custom, and chance. In the successful marriage this seems to work quite well, Jim knowing it is his business to take care of the family finances and Lena looking after her area of responsibility by making their social plans, and so on. Perhaps in some areas a certain amount of discontent arises when Lena thinks Jim has taken some liberties where her own territory is concerned, or where Lena engages in some major expenditure without checking this out with Jim. But, in their good relationship, these problems are not important and, in any case, neither feels that there are rigid demarcations to be observed.

What Jim and Lena have managed is to arrive at an unspoken agreement about who takes care of what, but they stay pretty flexible about the matter. They achieved this state of affairs quite naturally and would probably claim, if we asked them, that they both feel responsible for everything that happens. There is no written agreement, nor have they ever felt the need to sit down together and work out a plan about who does what; their understanding is not recorded in any way but it seems to work smoothly. Not everyone is so fortunate, and difficulties surrounding decision-making are among the most common of relationship problems.

Making plans is a first step in dealing with such problems, so that a conscious effort is made to examine what is done and what changes are needed. What Jim and Lena seem to have done quite naturally and without fuss, the distressed couple will need to do in a more thoughtful and deliberate fashion.

MAKE PLANS

As a guide to understanding just how you and your partner reach decisions in some important aspects of your life together, and what changes you would like to see, complete the checlists (pp. 102 to 105). The first list concerns what you and your partner believe is the present pattern of decision-making, while the second has to do with the changes you would like to make in this respect. By using different color pens to record your checks it will be easy to see where you agree and disagree. Don't regard disagreement as a cause for concern but as information to better appreciate how your partner sees matters.

KEEF

Clinging to authority

DON'T SEEK OR CLING TO AUTHORITY FOR ITS OWN SAKE

Lois and Paul disagree strongly about education for the children. Lois feels they should pay for private education to secure the best possible chance for them, while Paul feels they ought to survive the state educational system. If they've got it in them, he claims, it will come out OK. In fact Paul rather looks on this area as his own province, believing that he knows much more about this sort of thing than Lois. But he also thinks of it as a whole lot more *important* than the price of potatoes — which is Lois's business. Paul likes this area of authority, and part of his difficulty in sharing it with Lois comes from his possessiveness about 'important' matters.

Paul clings to this area of authority for its own sake and doesn't really want to share it with Lois. He justifies this in terms of his greater expertise in the area, but it is not a very sound claim and in any case, Lois has taken a lot of trouble to get at the facts. That she wants some say in the matter should be enough and Paul must 'give' on this issue.

SKILL AND COMPETENCE SHOULD COUNT

Power-sharing on a particular issue could, of course, be silly and inefficient if it is simply for its own sake. One or other partner might well feel much more comfortable exercising authority in a particular area, or may have a degree of expertise that would seem to justify having a greater share of influence in the matter. The rule here must be that it is with the *consent* of one partner that the other takes on a particular decision-making task, as well as keeping the other partner properly informed.

Rex has Evelyn as both his wife and business partner. As a highly intelligent and personable individual, she very quickly learned how to manage that part of the business which became her special responsibility. Together they have built a successful company but, always, Rex kept a firm overall control that Evelyn came to resent more and more as the years passed. In fact, he kept a good many things about their joint enterprise entirely to himself; Evelyn felt she was left out of some important decisions that had been made, and that Rex was deliberately preventing her from sharing fully. On many occasions she had tried to signal her discontent, but Rex either didn't notice or didn't want to solve the problem. The matter finally came to a head when Rex announced that they were selling out to a national company. It was, in a way, a good deal and a fine financial reward for their efforts, but Evelyn refused to go along with the plan. Afterwards, Rex admitted his error but, by this time, the problem had blossomed into major conflicts that affected every facet of their lives.

It was certainly true that Rex's expertise had got the business started and, at that stage, Evelyn had acknowledged this and allowed a pattern of authority to develop which later became unacceptable. Neither made any allowance for the professional

HOW ARE DECISIONS MADE IN THE FOLLOWING AREAS?	BY HUSBAND	BY WIFE	BY BOTH	MAINLY HUSBAND	MAINLY WIFE
1. Where to live	☐	☐	☐	☐	☐
2. Move to new house or neighborhood	☐	☐	☐	☐	☐
3. Purchase of furniture and decorations	☐	☐	☐	☐	☐
4. Politics and voting	☐	☐	☐	☐	☐
5. Type of work husband does	☐	☐	☐	☐	☐
6. Type of work wife does	☐	☐	☐	☐	☐
7. Home chores by husband	☐	☐	☐	☐	☐
8. What wife does at home	☐	☐	☐	☐	☐
9. Children's education	☐	☐	☐	☐	☐
10. Children's discipline	☐	☐	☐	☐	☐
11. Children's activities	☐	☐	☐	☐	☐
12. Amount of 'say' children have	☐	☐	☐	☐	☐
13. Who takes children to clubs, activities, etc.	☐	☐	☐	☐	☐
14. Who helps children with homework	☐	☐	☐	☐	☐
15. Payment of bills	☐	☐	☐	☐	☐
16. How to spend surplus money	☐	☐	☐	☐	☐
17. How to save for the future	☐	☐	☐	☐	☐
18. About life insurance	☐	☐	☐	☐	☐
19. When and how to have sex	☐	☐	☐	☐	☐

20. Size of family □ □ □ □ □

21. Gifts to charity □ □ □ □ □

22. Where and when to spend holidays □ □ □ □ □

23. How to spend leisure time □ □ □ □ □

24. Type of social activities □ □ □ □ □

25. What clubs and organizations to join □ □ □ □ □

26. Selection of friends □ □ □ □ □

27. Visits to and contact with relatives □ □ □ □ □

28. Giving presents □ □ □ □ □

29. When to seek professional advice □ □ □ □ □

30. What newspapers and magazines are bought □ □ □ □ □

31. What TV programes are viewed □ □ □ □ □

32. Diet and type of food consumed □ □ □ □ □

33. Making excuses when backing out of arrangements □ □ □ □ □

34. Dealing with difficult neighbors □ □ □ □ □

35. Making complaints about poor service, broken equipment, etc. □ □ □ □ □

36. Shopping purchases of everyday goods □ □ □ □ □

37. Making the 'difficult' phone call □ □ □ □ □

38. Religious matters/church attendance □ □ □ □ □

39. 'Making up' after a quarrel □ □ □ □ □

40. Making sure significant dates are remembered □ □ □ □ □

WHAT CHANGES WOULD YOU LIKE TO SEE IN DECISION-MAKING?

	MAINLY HUSBAND	MAINLY WIFE	MORE SHARING
1. Where to live	☐	☐	☐
2. Move to new house or neighborhood	☐	☐	☐
3. Purchase of furniture and decorations	☐	☐	☐
4. Politics and voting	☐	☐	☐
5. Type of work husband does	☐	☐	☐
6. Type of work wife does	☐	☐	☐
7. Home chores by husband	☐	☐	☐
8. What wife does at home	☐	☐	☐
9. Children's education	☐	☐	☐
10. Children's discipline	☐	☐	☐
11. Children's activities	☐	☐	☐
12. Amount of 'say' children have	☐	☐	☐
13. Who takes children to clubs, activities, etc.	☐	☐	☐
14. Who helps children with homework	☐	☐	☐
15. Payment of bills	☐	☐	☐
16. How to spend surplus money	☐	☐	☐
17. How to save for the future	☐	☐	☐
18. About life insurance	☐	☐	☐
19. When and how to have sex	☐	☐	☐

20. Size of family ☐ ☐ ☐

21. Gifts to charity ☐ ☐ ☐

22. Where and when to spend holidays ☐ ☐ ☐

23. How to spend leisure time ☐ ☐ ☐

24. Type of social activities ☐ ☐ ☐

25. What clubs and organizations to join ☐ ☐ ☐

26. Selection of friends ☐ ☐ ☐

27. Visits to and contact with relatives ☐ ☐ ☐

28. Giving presents ☐ ☐ ☐

29. When to seek professional advice ☐ ☐ ☐

30. What newspapers and magazines are bought ☐ ☐ ☐

31. What TV programs are viewed ☐ ☐ ☐

32. Diet and type of food consumed ☐ ☐ ☐

33. Making excuses when backing out of arrangements ☐ ☐ ☐

34. Dealing with difficult neighbors ☐ ☐ ☐

35. Making complaints about poor service, broken equipment, etc. ☐ ☐ ☐

36. Shopping purchases of everyday goods ☐ ☐ ☐

37. Making the 'difficult' phone call ☐ ☐ ☐

38. Religious matters/church attendance ☐ ☐ ☐

39. 'Making up' after a quarrel ☐ ☐ ☐

40. Making sure significant dates are remembered ☐ ☐ ☐

growth that Evelyn would undergo, and what began as a reasonable arrangement soon became outmoded. What Rex and Evelyn should have done was to continue to share authority according to the expertise each brought to the business, altering this arrangement to recognize Evelyn's growing skills and, above all, to make their sharing an open rather than the closed system that Rex made it.

It is appropriate that expertise and special ability play a part – the one with the head for figures does the accounts – but only with the consent and general understanding of the other partner.

PLAY IT STRAIGHT

It is all too easy for one or other partner to behave like Paul or Rex in the examples given, concealing their real motives for hanging on to power in a particular area. It is quite simple, too, for one partner to keep 'hidden' some of the information that lies behind the decision to do this or that, and Evelyn's reaction is as much to what she senses is going on behind the scenes as to what she actually discovers. Sometimes, too, one partner may keep back information which affects a decision that the other may have to make, exerting a hidden influence over the issue as the following case shows.

For some time Laura had been in the habit of 'creaming off' small amounts of her housekeeping budget and putting this into a savings account. It had started with the idea of giving the family a nice surprise one day, perhaps taking them all on a holiday they thought they couldn't afford. But, as time went on, she felt it was a pity just to waste her hard-won savings in this way and so just let the account go on building up. Even when Terry ran into repayment problems on the video, Laura didn't declare the savings account.

Good, effective decision-making involves trust and confidence in your partner – and a commitment to frankness in saying what you would like as your decision-making responsibilities, and why you want them.

MAKING CHANGES IN THE DECISION PATTERN

The checklist you have completed will give a start to your task of making changes. From this list you will be able to compare your own ideas with those of your partner and then begin to arrange the new deals that will be satisfactory to both. The general guidelines to making the deals are those set out above, and are summarized here:

1. To examine what you are doing at the moment and make modifications to meet your partner's wishes.
2. To recognize experience, expertise, and personal preferences in making your deals.
3. To avoid hanging on to authority for its own sake.
4. To make the exercise of authority and responsibility an open matter.
5. To deal honestly with your partner.

You will need to add to the list to suit the particular circumstances in your own lives and you will need to go into the practical details involved in contentious issues, for example:

Who drives home after the party.
Who cleans the car.
Who makes the excuses to the unwelcome guest.

In the failing relationship there are usually a number of major discrepancies, both as to who *actually does* what and who *should do* what. These differences have to be dealt with in the ways outlined in the chapters on communication and conflict (Chapters 4 and 5), namely by setting aside discussion time, keeping to the relevant issue, not personalizing the matter, being specific about what you want, and so on.

DON'T JUST STAND THERE COMPLAINING

Zoe was infuriated by Leo's tendency to opt out of disciplining the children. She felt it was always up to her to make them sit properly at meals, to be polite, to wash, to get to bed in reasonable time, and to be responsible for just about all other ways in which authority was exercised with them. Leo played football with them, took them swimming, and played a full part in what Zoe thought of as 'the entertainment bit', but she felt Leo not only had the easy part but also came high in the popularity polls, since she had to get the kids to do all the things they really didn't want to do. But she did nothing about this except complain and,

Choosing your time to communicate

somehow, Leo was never able to see how he could help. He saw himself as a good father and couldn't understand what he was doing wrong; in fact, he wasn't doing anything wrong, but he *was* failing to take on his share in disciplining the kids.

Zoe's job is to stop complaining and focus on what it is that she feels needs to be changed. She should be positive in her approach to Leo, saying 'I want to talk about how we deal with the children. We need to get clear what is wrong with their behavior, what action to take about this and who it is that will take that action. Can we discuss it tonight, please?' Zoe should not attempt to embark upon an agreement that simply passes all the child discipline work over to Leo; what she needs is an agreement that will satisfy **both** partners. It is the agreed redistribution of authority that is the object of their discussions; it is the *equitable*, but *not necessarily equal* sharing of power that is being sought.

TIMING THE DISCUSSION

Just as it is important to 'set the scene' in conflict reduction, so it is essential to making satisfactory changes to decision-making that the partners create an appropriate climate for this. Choose a time when you both can sit down in a relaxed way without distractions or interruptions. Be close to each other physically and help create a relaxed atmosphere by having a drink. Take the changes to be made just one at a time, not trying to hurry along solutions but, rather, making sure that you arrive at workable arrangements. Go into the discussions with the sole idea of getting a mutually agreeable answer to the problem.

Remember, it is an open and free discussion between you, so you don't need to be inhibited about what *you* see as the right answer. Nor should your suggestions be called into question or ridiculed – they are your honestly expressed ideas about change. You must also see your partner's ideas as expressing his or her own honest opinions and not as crazy notions to be attacked. Between you, compromise is to be achieved – not necessarily a 50/50 agreement, but a new balance which leaves both partners satisfied, and not feeling that one or the other got all their own way.

GETTING IT RIGHT

Putting your side of the case in an acceptable way is something of an art. Most couples with good relationships have mastered this skill but very few failing partnerships have managed to do so. See if you can spot the right and wrong ways of doing things in the following example.

Donna is very keen to get the living room looking rather smarter and she raises this problem with Jonathan:

'How about getting your den cleaned up this weekend?'

This is *wrong* because her real objective is to move on to the lounge, and her suggestion of tidying Jonathan's den is softening him up. Donna has to be more direct and open about what she wants a decision on.

Here is another approach:

'Jonathan, should we get the living room redecorated or shall we buy a new carpet?'

This is wrong too, because Donna hasn't given any real choice to Jonathan – it's not so much a discussion now as an ultimatum. Donna should be opening up the debate to find out *how Jonathan feels* about the general problem of smartening up the living room.

As the conversation progresses Jonathan begins to get anxious:

'Can't we get along without either, you know things are a bit tight just now and we've got a lot of bills to face next month.'

This is wrong too. Jonathan isn't really talking about Donna's idea so much as telling her it can't be done. Although she has presented only two possibilities, he *could* have told her it is really a very good idea, agree the room looks pretty shabby, and that in a couple of months they could probably have enough money saved to consider the first possibility.

Donna doesn't see things well either at this stage, so she turns to her usual tactic when feeling frustrated:

'Why do you always have to turn down everything I suggest . . . I work so hard to make things look nice . . . you never seem to appreciate it . . . etc.'

The reasons that she is wrong again here are obvious. First, she is not sticking to the issue and trying to get a real discussion going, but turning to irrelevancies and generalizations, becoming emotional and about to give Jonathan a history lesson about his failings.

A much better way of having the same discussion would be as follows:

Donna: 'The living room is getting to look a bit shabby these days, maybe you feel the same about it. It seems like a good idea to have that old carpet replaced, or maybe we could even think of a complete repaint job. The old carpet might raise a bit of cash if we sold it and we could send a few other things to the sale rooms while we are about it. What do you think?'
Jonathan: 'Well, I guess it all looks in need of a face lift . . . maybe we ought to do something about it . . . but we don't have a lot of spare money right now. What do you think it would all cost?'
Donna: 'I saw a beautiful carpet in the store last week, but it certainly was expensive . . . I'm sure I can find something really

nice at a more reasonable price . . . I'll look around and get some prices. I can also find the cost of getting a repaint and bring along some color schemes for us to look at.'

HONESTY IS THE BEST POLICY

Both Donna and Jonathan have set about making a deal on this matter which, so far as both are concerned, is really Donna's territory. Jonathan is to be consulted and kept informed, but he is simply going to be supportive of what Donna wants so long as this doesn't wreck their finances. Furthermore, they didn't personalize or emotionalize the problem, nor did Donna try to steamroller the decision through, although she badky wants to have the thing settled.

She could be tempted, at their next chance to talk it over, to present a false account of her fact-finding mission. She could underplay the price of the new carpet (because this is what *she* really sees as the solution to the problem) by quoting the cost of the less attractive version. Later, when she takes Jonathan along to the store to see it for himself, he will have to agree that the economy finish is not good enough and the color is wrong too; with luck he will agree to spend more than he wanted to because Donna has already committed him to buying a new carpet anyway. Here the true nature of the 'deal' only becomes evident later.

Jonathan can use the same trick when it comes to joining the golf club. After all, you *can* get a set of clubs for as little as X, but it won't be the set of clubs he wants to own. So, the 'deal' is made, Donna giving approval to his plan without knowing the true cost. Also, he didn't tell her that he'd like to play in matches that would take him away from home on quite a few weekends and attend a few international tournaments, whereas Donna thought of it as an occasional Sunday morning exercise with a set of inexpensive clubs.

THE FILIBUSTER

The aims of discussions on power and authority are to describe the present state, to tell your partner about the changes you want to have, and to come to some mutually agreed conclusions. It is the second aim that often produces the most problems since, as we have seen, there can be coercion to reach a conclusion or distortion to ensure things are seen the way one would prefer. A further problem arises from the disparity between the partners in their ability to put the case, and it is sometimes found that the wordy and highly articulate individual has the advantage.

In these circumstances, the less verbal partner may be persuaded to make a deal that, on reflection, is not a good one at all. Here, both partners must show a willingness to have a re-run of the discussion in the light of subsequent events, not taking the view that once the deal has been made it becomes sacrosanct.

More often, however, one of the partners is able to stretch out the discussions until the other gives in simply from boredom or exhaustion. Talking your partner out is a failing strategy and bound to lead to discontent, even if successful on a temporary basis.

COMMON PROBLEMS IN DECISION-MAKING

THE STING

Freda asked Malcolm for his opinion about having Jeanette take ballet lessons, saying 'She's just about the right age to start now and she's so keen to go with her friends.' Malcolm isn't too sure about this way of spending money and suggests maybe they could put off considering this for another year. Freda reacts badly and starts to yell at him that he reduces everything to money.

It would have been much better if Freda had anticipated Malcolm's reaction and had told him that she had been thinking of taking a part-time job to help out with payments. Furthermore, just keeping up with Jeanette's friends isn't so convincing an argument and if Freda had (genuinely) thought that Jeanette had real talent, or would be able to enjoy new opportunities, then Malcolm could perhaps have given more thought to the matter. But Freda didn't offer anything except satisfying Jeanette's wish to take ballet, and they got sidetracked from the main problem by her outburst.

A more successful way of dealing with the same issue would involve:

1. A clear statement of the problem.
2. Some anticipation of any snags or difficulties – Freda

shouldn't just expect complete agreement to any idea she puts forward.

3. A few notions about how any difficulties can be got around.

In fact there shouldn't be any reaction from Freda simply because Malcolm feels the plan would be better put off for a time; she has no right to Malcolm's instant agreement. Nor should there be any brinkmanship about the way in which points are put, where one or other partner raises the tempo of the discussion to make any disagreement a matter of ctitical significance.

Ted and Barbara were discussing the people to invite to their son's wedding. They had checked the bride's list and felt they should have just about the same number of people from their side. Unfortunately, by the time they'd compiled their list, it was far too top-heavy and some trimming was needed. Barbara and Ted couldn't see eye-to-eye on who should be cut, and Barbara 'catastrophized' the matter by saying that if they left out such-and-such a person she simply couldn't go to any social function again where that individual would be around. Barbara was using this as a *way* of getting Ted to drop someone *he* wanted, or she would make their social life difficult.

NOT FEELING REJECTED

In the examples of Donna and Jonathan and of Malcolm and Freda, Donna goes back to her old strategy of 'Why do you turn down everything I mention . . .' and Freda makes it difficult for Malcolm to reject her idea by threats of catastrophe. Donna feels rejected because she set a lot of store by her idea and badly wants to put it into action; really, she is insisting that Jonathan should go along with it unquestioningly. Freda also feels like turning any opposition into a rejection of her and her ideas. Both girls overstate the problems and introduce an emotional and over dramatic note into the discussion. They must understand that disagreement does not mean rejection, each partner having a perfect right to say what he or she thinks on the issue, without threats to pull out of discussions or get into a fight. There should be no penalties for opposing viewpoints.

THE NON-SERIOUS DISCUSSANT

In the chapters relating to communication and conflict it has been pointed out that there is a temptation to use discussions for purely personal motives and to manipulate these sessions to achieve personal ends and objectives. In arrangements about decision-making, the tendency in some cases to hide the true cost of decisions, to filibuster, and to operate the 'sting' have been mentioned.

To add to these we must note the 'irrelevant leverage' and the 'who, me?' gambits.

IRRELEVANT LEVERAGE

Wayne is quite fond of this strategy since it usually works very well with Zena. He can play this very convincingly because she has a lot of trust in his judgment, as a man of the world. Their discussions are liberally sprinkled with Wayne's 'We both want the same thing really, don't we . . .' or 'Let's face up to the thing squarely . . .', giving the impression that he's coming at least halfway to meeting her already. 'We both want the best for the children' is not unlike the used-car salesman's 'You really want a reliable car, don't you sir?' Since no one wants an unreliable car it is hoped that the next statement following will look like a logical consequence. The logical connection is actually missing, but often this is not noticed.

THE 'WHO ME?' GAMBIT

Another problem is that an agreement, when reached, is later retracted by 'You must have misunderstood me' or, if pressed, 'Maybe I didn't make myself clear.' Always, of course, there is room for misunderstandings, but the non-serious discussant is frequently guilty of turning his or her back upon agreements reached and denying that any arrangement was made, or claiming that the other person misunderstood what was said. Indeed, the individual skilled in denial is often good at making any question asked about the agreement sound like paranoia or yet another example of the other person not really listening properly.

It is not only annoying to the partner who felt that an understanding *had* been reached, but the 'Who, me?' gambit also makes future agreements difficult to reach because confidence and trust is lost.

There is no substitute for both partners seeing clearly that open discussion and honesty are essential to good relationships, but there are a few things that can be done by the 'victim' when the purpose of discussions has been undermined in some way.

1. Despite an inclination to lose one's temper, become accusatory or just give up, the rule is to re-open the discussion.
2. Do so in a non-accusatory way – don't begin by saying 'You made a mess of . . .' or 'You didn't pay any attention to our agreement . . .', etc.
3. Don't go over the remiss behavior of your partner, just go back to discussing the matter that was thought to have been agreed.
4. Don't be apologetic about re-opening the discussion. Just keep your mind on the main objective of improving your relationship. It is in your interests to do so.
5. Approach the re-opening of the discussion with confidence, setting aside any idea of your pride being at stake or of getting your own back.

If you stick to your guns, behave with forebearance, and deal honestly with your partner, you will reap the benefits.

SUMMARY OF POINTS IN THIS CHAPTER

1. Don't aim at 50/50 solutions but sensible ones that take account of real expertise, time available, and personal preference.
2. Be planful: make your list of decision problems and discuss properly, using the rules for communication and conflict-avoidance.
3. Be honest, play it straight. Don't use subterfuge to get your way, or any of the misguided tactics referred to.
4. Don't use your discussion sessions to complain; be constructive.
5. Put your case in the appropriate positive way, offer alternatives, think the matter through, and listen to your partner.
6. Don't become emotional or quit the situation. Stay with the discussion, re-opening it as necessary, until you have an agreement.
7. Don't look for perfection in your agreements but something you can both accept and live with.
8. Don't feel rejected if you don't get exactly what you want or don't get an immediate acceptance of your ideas by your partner. Discussions are not held to give you just what *you* want, but to explore how each of you can change your behavior and reach a new understanding.

CHAPTER 7

How to Make the Most of your Relationship

It is easier to get a license to marry than to pass a driving test. Not, of course, that a driving license prevents accidents, but we hope that some test of competence to drive will keep down the casualty figures. No display of competence at all is required before people marry and, for this reason alone, we should not be surprised by the casualty figures. Indeed, in many marriages the crash comes all too quickly. Whereas before marriage the couple may have tended to treat each other as special people, with most aspects of their contact being pleasurable, after marriage this tends to undergo a marked change. It is as if, having reached some desired goal, there is nowhere left to go, the couple failing to see that marriage is a new beginning rather than an end in itself.

In fact many couples do not see that their relationship is going to need the kind of attention and care that one would bring (at the very least) to keeping a car in repair or the house in good decorative order. There is a lack of recognition that the relationship will need effort to avoid inevitable drift, decline, and decay. For them, the mere act of entering marriage is thought to be enough and, the ceremony over, they feel ready to relax and savour the pure enjoyments of having achieved a desired end.

The drift into complacency, with its conception that marriage, once undertaken, will run forever sweetly and problem-free, must be checked. So, too, must the notion that any partnership will remain forever in its original form, static and undisturbed by time and life's difficulties. In fact, quite opposite attitudes will be required, calling for effort and constant attention to the needs of a growing, dynamic, evolving, and changing relationship.

Some of the influences that will demand changes from us are well known, such as losing the support of parents, having children, becoming menopausal, or retirement from work. But other more subtle changes constantly take place that we need to anticipate and adjust to, allowing our relationship to grow and mature in these new circumstances. Nothing stays the same and we must learn to see the evolution of our married lives as a challenge and opportunity for enhancement, rather than as a source of problems.

Some of the phases that we pass through can be seen as the quite natural result of biological or social forces of an expected kind. They are 'normal' and can be anticipated and dealt with. Other changes come unexpectedly and are often more damaging and brutal. A few of these major problems are now looked at briefly before examining how we may begin to appreciate the positive ways in which we can enhance our marriages and avoid complacency.

ILLNESS IN MARRIAGE

It is clear that the chances for a marriage to evolve to mature and to progress with time, vary greatly with circumstances. The physical illness of a partner, especially of a lengthy and debilitating kind, can produce grave problems for the survival of the marriage, and coping with such difficulties is not always within the capacity of either partner. Although some do make the necessary adjustments to the limitations imposed and manage cheerfully to carry the burdens and sacrifices involved, a lot depends on the personality of those involved. Not all sick individuals bear their problems with fortitude and consideration for others, and not all well partners are tolerant of the immense drain on their resources. Indeed, keeping one's balance in such circumstances is probably achieved by a minority rather than the majority.

Mental illness as well as physical can be an enormous source of stress and even the lesser forms of psychological disturbance pose a serious threat to relationships. Whatever the form of

Bearing the burden of illness with fortitude

disability, the sick partner is going to need a good deal more help, support, and understanding than a stable and healthy individual. Such burdens add substantially to the existing problems of relationships.

There is little that we can do, before marriage, to anticipate the problems of illness. Although a few couples enter their partnership in the knowledge of major illness being a probability, for most the outcome will hinge crucially on the character and resolve of the individuals concerned.

LOOKING FOR SOMEONE NEW

Mike had left Penny many times. Eventually, as she knew from long experience, his latest 'escapade' would come to an end and he would return to the family home, smiling sheepishly and playing the part of the naughty schoolboy who deserved nothing but mild reproof. In any case, by now, he was quite confident that Penny would have him back – she always did, even if it meant putting up with her sulks for a while. As Penny ruefully pointed out, he had been this way from the beginning; in fact her friends had warned her about it and advised against marrying him. But then Penny had thought that all Mike needed was real love and the right kind of woman, and it was only now that she could see how wrong she had been. To Penny it seemed that she'd made her bed and would have to lie in it, often alone.

Mike, a tall, handsome, and charming 48-year-old, shows little sign of changing or, for that matter, of genuine contrition. Indeed, he makes no pretence about remaining faithful for very long and, from time to time, points out to Penny that he just can't help it – he's just *made* that way. If Penny gets too upset and, on occasion, rejects him, he can put on a dramatic performance, declaring that he has never really loved anyone except Penny and will truly make a real effort to reform. It is hard to know whether Penny believes this at the time, although she badly wants to do so and she manages to carry on as if Mike had undergone his conversion.

Mike is a professional man with a large and successful practice. He is good at his job, highly popular, generous and courteous in his dealings with others in public settings; in his private life with Penny he inflicts great suffering on her and the children. But the kids, now in their early twenties, have grown cynical about human relationships and, to an extent, have become hardened to their father's wayward life.

Penny's friends are irritated by her behavior. They feel she should have listened to their warnings and, even though she went ahead with the marriage, she should have left him long ago rather than go on putting up with his inexcusable conduct. Indeed, although we may guess that there is more than meets the eye to Penny's willingness to continue tolerating the insufferable, the reason for her inaction remains a mystery.

The research evidence is heavily in favor of Penny's friends. Getting married does *not* cure existing difficulties, and we are wise to take note of this in selecting our partners. Indeed, pro-marriage difficulties have a strong tendency to continue and will add to all the other problems that stem, quite naturally, from the decision to share our lives with someone else.

Like a naughty schoolboy

Alan, in some ways, might be thought to be an unfortunate victim of the need to find new relationships. He became restless and irritated by the 'boredom' of his marriage and, after some thought, persuaded Jenny that a special relationship with another couple would do quite a lot to revitalize their own relationship. After all, she must agree, their life together had become a rather tedious and predictable thing and provided no real excitement at all. At first reluctant, Jenny finally agreed and for a few weeks the plan worked very well. It was not, however, that Alan and Jenny's relationship was being revitalized, but that the novelty and clandestine nature of partner-swapping did lend a decidedly new and thrilling touch to their lives. The pleasure was short-lived. After a few months Jenny had decided that Peter was in many ways a far more desirable partner and left to live with him, taking the children with her. Oddly, although utterly distraught at losing his wife, his children, and part of his home, Alan still thinks of his idea as being basically sound.

Such mistakes are now commonplace and, sadly, reflect the inability of the people concerned to create and maintain effective and stable relationships with each other – or anyone else, for that matter. The chances of these individuals actually finding fulfilment in new partne ships is reduced rather than increased by their actions, as they have not examined their problems, nor devised workable solutions to them, but have avoided dealing with issues and, instead, have engaged in irrelevant strategies. No thought has been given to enhancing the relationship they already have in order to secure greater satisfaction but, rather, the old partnership has been discarded in a way one might think would be more suited to dealing with worn-out machinery.

It could be argued that some of the difficulties mentioned could have been avoided before marriage was considered. Certainly, Penny could have listened to advice about Mike and, surely, Alan's dissatisfaction with just one ongoing sexual relationship would have been detectable. It is notable, however, that in both these cases, marriage took place shortly after the couples first met and this may be a clue to where the mistake was made – each had a very incomplete picture of the other. A good rule, although not one to depend on too greatly, is to spend time in careful evaluation of prospective partners – common sense, perhaps, but not a precaution taken too often these days.

CULTURAL AND RELIGIOUS INFLUENCES

Ann, despite very strong opposition from her parents, first lived with and then married an Arab student. To Ann, living with her rather 'old-fashioned' parents in a small provincial town, her boyfriend studying at the local university radiated romance. Ahmed was attentive, courteous, and lavished gifts on her in fits of unusual extravagance. Ann's parents refused to attend the wedding which took place just after her eighteenth birthday and, even more disappointing to Ann, no representative of Ahmed's family came to the ceremony.

She saw nothing at all wrong in adopting her husband's faith and, indeed, saw it as of no real importance. After all, they now had each other and, to her, a new and highly exciting life in Ahmed's own country the following year was a delightful and romantic prospect. But, as it turned out, Ahmed's studies were not completed, since he failed to comply with the regulations for his engineering course. To add to their problems Ann was now pregnant and the couple decided that the time had come to leave for Ahmed's homeland.

Ann's initial shock at the squalid conditions of the house that she was to share with the numerous members of Ahmed's family was profound. It seemed so totally at odds with the vision she had entertained and, to make matters worse, only one of her husband's brothers spoke a little English, and her sense of isolation became acute. The climate, too, was unbearable and it became clear that ante- and post-natal care were going to be serious problems.

Matters came to a head when Ahmed's behavior, triggered by Ann's complaints, changed to being autocratic and angry. Life became more oppressive and, to add to her misery, she was not allowed to leave the house without Ahmed's permission.

The story can be told many times over, the essential ingredient being the mistaken belief that cultural factors are unimportant. It was not just that Ann's view of her Arabic home had been too romantic and wildly inaccurate, but that she was totally unprepared for differences in manners, customs, language, food, amenities, and just about everything else.

Pauline made a similar discovery after marrying a man from a Central African State. Mabindi's stories about his homeland and his family's importance gave Pauline a distorted view of what life would be like as his wife. It was true that, once in Africa, they enjoyed a privileged position in beautiful rural surroundings, but life was hardly glamorous. Pauline found a total absence of all the things she had taken for granted back home, including clean running water and toilet facilities. Indeed, life was monotonous and squalid and it became clear that the family's position was politically vulnerable. Repeated pregnancies increased her distress (although she was afraid to complain in case she was beaten according to local custom) and she fled, leaving her children behind.

Although extreme, such cases are not unusual and accurately reflect the well-documented problems that can arise when cultural boundaties are crossed. To the girls concerned, the behavior of their husbands was cruel and deceitful, but it is also true that there was total blindness on their part to cultural problems – and perhaps some degree of self-deception.

More subtle cultural boundaries are crossed with less dire consequences. Indeed, it is worth noting that some individuals make the transition well and readily adapt to the demands of new values and standards. But they remain a loading against finding marital adjustment, and those who thoughtlessly cross these boundaries will often become casualties. The rewards of marriage are not easily won and to enter that state with an existing handicap is to take a serious risk.

Cynthia and Simon fell in love. He was from an orthodox Jewish family and Cynthia was a Gentile. Many attempts to prevent the marriage going ahead were made, but Simon went through with the civil ceremony and things went well for a couple of years. Totally rejected by his family, Simon began to regret the loss and the barrier that had come between him and his friends. Eventually he made new contact with his parents, although they still remained critical of Cynthia and refused to accept her as their daughter-in-law. Understandably, she felt humiliated and rejected and Simon's behavior seemed to add to her sense of betrayal. Their relationship became a sad parody of two years ago but, to Simon's parents, the discord was the proof of what they had always believed.

To the young, differences in religion seem only to be small obstacles and the danger signals are weak and disregarded. One could say how right Ann's parents were to object to her marriage, and how sensible Simon's parents were to try and dissuade him, although even they might feel disappointment that the outcome was as they had predicted. Some relationships do survive – and flourish – when major religious or cultural boundaries are violated, but it is unwise to assume that they do not matter.

DIFFERENCES IN AGE

Age differences seem to be rather less important as a source of difficulty and, by and large, discrepancies of 10–15 years have little influence. It is probable, however, that age only becomes an important factor later in life and during the early years of a relationship the difference is not especially noticeable. While a wife of 20 may find a man of 35 entirely compatible and, indeed, discover in him someone of experience, of settled nature, and comparative affluence, the same lady at 50 may have a partner who has become inactive, in less good health, and now living on a retirement pension. It is easy, too, to see how the young children of the 50-year-old father may take a different view of such an individual than they would of the 30-year-old man who won the Father's Race at the school sports day. Family responsibilities and changes in physical and psychological status will inevitably make continued adjustment more of a problem for the age-discrepant couple.

DIFFERENCES IN EDUCATION AND INTELLIGENCE

Differences in education and intellectual level do not always become a cause of marital discord and may rarely serve as the main cause, yet they do exercise an influence. Again, such matters are generally regarded by those with strong emotional attachments as being of little real consequence and it is only in time that the weight of such differences becomes apparent.

John has achieved a high position in his company. His job involves a good deal of travel and much of his key work is in social settings. His intelligence, natural charm, and strong personality carry him through these situations well, but Esther is intimidated by them. In fact she has always been rather shy and, with her lack of formal education, she feels stupidly tongue-tied on some social occasions that are critical to John's job. John keeps her out of the picture as much as possible these days, but he feels a sense of frustration and anger that he lacks the support that others seem to get from their wives. Secretly, he is ashamed of Esther who, although still quite pretty for her age, no longer fulfils the new role John's wife must occupy.

Daphne entertains similar feelings to those that John has about his wife. They arise in a different context since Daphne isn't a captain of industry but someone who has become increasingly involved in local cultural and artistic pursuits. This is only in her own small city, but it brings her into proximity with people who know about literature, music, and painting and her husband, Sydney, knows nothing at all of such matters. It isn't that he remains silent about them either, because Sydney is a bluff, self-made man, given to speaking his mind, and he makes his contempt for art and culture very plain. He embarrasses Daphne by his frank display of ignorance and she feels that she made a mistake in marrying someone so insensitive.

In both John and Daphne's cases, it is probable that their differences in outlook, in personality, and in ambition were already present before marriage. The adjustments needed to grow more closely together might have been made, but this did not happen. Instead, each couple grew further apart and more aware of their differences until they reached a point where these outweighed the affection they had held for each other. Had John and Esther and Daphne and Sydney become more keenly aware of what the other would eventually want, they may still have believed that love would carry them through. On the other hand, it is possible that they would have considered that their differences in intellect, in education, or in aspiration, might become sources of distress.

Differences in personality, religion, culture, intelligence, and education are not precise yardsticks for labeling a partner as unsuitable yet, when such differences are substantial, they should at least serve as a caution. Generally, however, whatever risk factors of this kind exist, people tend to diminish their importance or feel that they will be able to overcome these obstacles. Nevertheless, it is recommended that couples should list their similarities and differences *before* marriage, perhaps seeking advice and help about any problems that might lie in wait.

MARRIAGE ENHANCEMENT

At the beginning of this book it was pointed out that divorce and separation have reached crisis proportions. This trend is now affecting one in two marriages in the USA and about one in three in Britain. In Europe generally, the picture is only a little better and, everywhere, the trend toward dissolution of marriage is upward.

These pages have provided strategies to help with those marriages that can be called distressed and which, without such help being given, would probably fail, This still leaves many marriages which survive although little is known about how many of these could be called truly happy or contented. Undoubtedly, the degree of happiness and satisfaction found ranges all the way from one extreme to the other. Some have become so unhappy that they are terminated, although it would appear that, these days, the tolerance level for things that go wrong has been lowered – couples deciding both earlier and on less provocation that the relationship is not working.

Few marriages are seen to be tragic mistakes from the very beginning. Instead, they seem to have gradually subsided into an unsatisfactory state, and it is during this decline that dealing with problems is important. It is clear that the process of deterioration in relationships *can* be halted – or at least slowed down – if a determined attempt is made to strengthen them. This process has been called 'marriage enhancement' and refers to the continuous monitoring and servicing of a relationship to prevent those involved becoming complacent, static, or just plain disagreeable. It is something that all couples must consider, whether or not distress is being experienced in the relationship, and a regular review of the following suggestions is recommended.

DOING YOUR OWN THING

It will be apparent from several cases quoted in previous chapters that one or other partner sometimes makes the mistake of devoting himself or herself quite exclusively to the other's life plan. They offer themselves (more often the woman in the relationship) solely as a support and aid to the other person, realizing only at a late stage that this is not fully satisfying. The feelings of being redundant or simply an appendage to someone else's life

become more oppressive and urgent as the years pass, particularly when children become independent, perhaps leaving no clear
or useful role and function.

It is important to anticipate the need arising for an independent role quite distinct from that of your partner, which gives a
sense of fulfilment and personal contribution outside the relationship. This need not be greatly time-consuming, since the sole
purpose is to give a meaning and substance to the individual's life
that is not dependent upon a link with one's partner. Men are
usually more fortunate in that, more often, they have employment which offers them this independence and sense of useful-
ness. Women are less lucky and sometimes feel the need to take
on full-time employment in an exacting world to gain this sense
of independence. Often, husbands resent wives abandoning
their traditional role of caring for the family and difficulties arise,
but these problems can be put into perspective if both partners
appreciate that this special need to do one's own thing – to have
something of one's own to take pride in – is common to us all.
Couples will need to discuss this and to arrive (in ways described
earlier) at mutually agreed solutions to sharing, caring, and
independence.

It should not be thought that such a need is met always
through having paid employment outside the home. Voluntary
work or hobbies can offer just as much to the individual, although
this work is often viewed as being 'unimportant' or 'less serious'
by the uninformed.

DOING IT TOGETHER

Time for yourself to achieve something worthwhile is important,
but many couples tend to show a failing of quite the opposite
kind. The couple may be together but don't share their lives in
ways which would enhance the relationship.

Essentially, successful marriage is a matter of balance. As the
previous point emphasized, there has to be some part of one's life
that has a kind of separateness, but there must also be a part that
involves togetherness, a part for the family, a part for leisure, a
time for chores, and so on. The problem for most of us is that
these compartments to our partnerships are allowed just to
happen or – as is too often the case – simply not happen. A

conscious effort to **plan** how you share is essential if the opportunities are not going to be wasted. Here, one has in mind that the couple will arrange some things that both enjoy, and that they can do those things together without feeling guilty about it. Having a meal out together, going to a concert or cinema, or just going out walking will do. Indeed, all that is required is that it is a shared time of pleasurable activity. Ideally this should happen once each week but, in any case, shouldn't be less than once each fortnight.

BEING ESPECIALLY NICE: THE EGO-BOOST

All of us tend to take our partners for granted at times, either forgetting to say and do those things that show how we really feel, or finding ourselves too busy and hoping our partners will know we still do care. This, in a good relationship, can go on for a long time without great harm, but even the best of marriages needs some positive feedback to keep the good feelings alive. What began as being simply too busy or forgetful can become a bad habit and dangerous neglect.

Accordingly, all couples should make a point of having days – or just evenings – for showing caring attitudes. If you feel it would all be rather stilted and contrived, then it shows how unused you are to displaying such attitudes! If you find it hard to think of quite what you might say or do on such caring occasions, then here are some suggestions:

1. If Sue has been feeling a bit low in spirits, then you set out to boost her morale. Tell her about her good points, flattering her a bit, and reminding her of the things she did that were great or really special.

2. If Tom has had a stressful time at work recently, then you can praise his good points, tell him how much you love him, say how good it is just to be with him, remind him of how much he's done for the kids, and so on.

3. Have a pleasant reminisce about the loving early days, put on some nice romantic music, break open the drinks cupboard, and get physically close.

4. Do something that you know your partner really likes. Maybe its a favorite food, getting in that special drink, a body massage, or a special way of having sex. Talk to him or her about it and have them get into a special mood about it.

Finally, why not exchange lists of nice things that you'd like to happen on these special days? Don't let your feelings that you might lose an advantage, or that it really isn't you, spoil your attempt to show the really strong positive feelings you can display.

KEEPING ROMANCE ALIVE

Related to the caring reactions described above is the need to keep a romantic side to your relationship. While it is true that a relationship passes from the purely romantic to one tinged by the realism of someone's dingy underwear, a heavy cold, just being too tired, crying kids, and so on, some place for romance has to be found. It is surprising how simple words like 'I love you' are received well and seen not just as old-fashioned sentiment. Leave a small message once a month in his socks or in her handbag saying 'I love you.' Give a small gift (however small) every month or so with a loving message. Make sure your sexual advances begin with a romantic expression – and end with one, too, not just curling up and going to sleep.

Try arranging a romantic evening now and then, just the two of you with your smoochy records, nice food, candlelight on the table (even the kitchen table will do, with a hamburger), but make a *special occasion* of it. Telephone at unexpected times just to say how much you care. Don't forget anniversaries and other special days.

Remember, promising yourself you'll get down to doing these things is not enough. Keep a 'diary' just marking the days that you will use as 'caring' or 'romantic.'

GROWING TOGETHER

Partners very often seem to experience some disappointment about the natural changes that occur. They feel that their partners should remain exactly the same through the years and sometimes, reproachfully, say 'He's changed . . . he's not the person I married 15 years ago.' Individuals *do* change and it can be for the better. Accepting change and allowing this force to bring you together, rather than seeing it as a barrier, is an important objective. Looking back at the enjoyment of discos or days of competitive sport may be pleasurably nostalgic, but enjoying the present is much more to the point, making the most of what, and who, you and your partner are right now.

From time to time, on a planned basis rather than leaving it to chance, every couple should sit down to talk about their lives together, their needs at the moment and their views of the future. Usually such reviews do not take place and often the partners find that they have moved apart rather than grown together.

But, just as important, is that couples should discuss the development and re-direction of their lives, not simply recounting the changes that are naturally occurring. The average couple simply do not contemplate *making* changes to their lives and, if asked, would be bewildered by the mere possibility. Yet some do so, perhaps leaving a comfortable suburban home to make a hazardous living from the land on a small island, set up their craft shop in a holiday community, or buy a bar in Barbados. Not all such ideas are good and, certainly, not all stand the test of time, but at least the possibility of making changes to a living pattern is being recognized. Most changes that a couple can usefully contemplate are far less dramatic and final than those mentioned, but they can be an immense source of re-energizing a relationship, restating a common purpose and commitment to staying together. Don't argue that you have no ideas or things are just 'too difficult' to consider change; at least sit down to exchange what *might* be done in a realistic and adventurous spirit.

HELPING DAYS

Alex never lifts a finger in the house. It isn't that he is a lazy man, as Wendy will readily admit, it's just that there are things that are down to Wendy and things down to himself. Household chores are Wendy's. Nor is it that Wendy needs so much help in the house; now the children are away she doesn't really have too much work and, if anything, she hasn't enough to fill her time. But Wendy does feel a kind of annoyance as she bustles about the house, seeing Alex stretched out on the sofa reading his newspapers.

She begins to find things for him to do by making complaints. It's Fall and she complains about the leaves that blow into the house whenever the door is opened; at least 'outside' is Alex's responsibility and if she nags enough he'll sigh, get up, and clear away the mess. He tells her that the leaves are going to fall for quite a while yet and the porch will be full of them again by this time tomorrow, but they both have missed the point. What Wendy is asking for is that Alex should show concern and interest in her by asking if he can help. In fact she may need to invent a little job or two for him, but that really doesn't matter, Alex is making himself into her helper.

Of course, if Alex had not created his work and responsibility divisions, he perhaps wouldn't have so big a problem. But, even if no such divisions had been made, it would be still important for him to make himself available to Wendy, and vice versa. These 'helping' times are not so much about being really useful as they are about showing affection. For those who are at fault in this respect it is difficult to make a beginning. To help you get started, set aside helping days in a deliberate way and use simple expressions of wanting to share, such as, 'What can I be doing while you're peeling the potatoes?' Later you may graduate to, 'I'll get the supper while you're busy with the ironing.'

WARTS AND ALL

'If you want to know me, come and live with me' is an adage that contains a lot of truth. It is all too easy in pre-marriage days to reveal only the more acceptable face of human relationships, and those physical intimacies rarely uncover the 'real' person underneath. Only when marriage or long-term relationships become consolidated do we begin to appreciate the true extent of the personal habits that didn't show up before, the degree to which priorities have changed, the requirement to share instead of the readiness to do so, the increased demand on our energy resources, and so on. The warts begin to show quite quickly and it is no great surprise to see how the early peak in divorce rates reflects this.

From the beginning, Delia says, Dale was a drunken bully and even her wedding night was a story of brutal physical assault. Did her husband really change so much at that time? Was there no warning sign beforehand? Did she provoke these attacks in any way?

Leslie, on the other hand, did not disclose to June that he had some obsessional habits and just hoped that, if they came to light, she would understand. Mavis married Harvey without telling him about her abnormal attitudes to food, she hoped he'd never find out that she had to vomit after eating a heavy meal.

It was wildly optimistic of Leslie and Mavis to think that their abnormal behavior could remain a secret or, that if they came to light, their partners would attach little significance to them. It is proper that partners should make such disclosures before marriage.

But much of what we are remains a private matter until the long-term relationship begins and only at that time do we become aware of how different we are from our partners. These differences are not often the gross abnormalities of Mavis and Leslie, yet they can and sometimes do stand out in a significant way in our partnerships. The rules about dealing with these minor differences are:

1. Don't set out to make changes in your partner when you have established your relationship. Accept him or her, warts and all, unless the differences are *really* going to get in the way.
2. If changes are to be discussed and examined, then choose those matters which are of real importance and not those which simply reflect a difference between you.
3. Have discussions and make the changes on an agreed basis, according to the rules set out earlier in this book.
4. It is necessary to be tolerant of many differences between you, and to see them as the reflection of your varied background experiences rather than as 'right ways' and 'wrong ways' of doing things.

TIME TO TALK

Felix and Josephine are nearing their fifties. Felix is a busy and successful GP while Josephine is on the local parole board and busy with her voluntary work with the homeless. They are intelligent and, in their special ways, quite effective people. They have a son and a daughter at University and a nice detached house in a leafy suburb. They have everything they want except for one thing: their relationship is one of emotional impoverishment, as if they've been so busy with the lives of other people that they had no time at all to attend to their own. They are now strangers to each other, meeting briefly over breakfast, or entertaining their professional friends to dinner, but their own relationship has, mysteriously and without their awareness, disappeared, leaving only the empty appearance of partnership. They talk, but it is the superficial exchange of views about their professional lives, their busy diaries, their commitments that allow or do not allow inviting the Jones's round. No meaningful exchange is left to them, no residual knowledge of those intimate feelings that they once shared.

Felix vaguely thinks they may be unsuited. Josephine, the recipient of a 'pass' by an elderly colleague, reflects momentarily upon separation. Both suppress these fragmentary glimpses of a relationship held together by convention rather than deep affection and respect, but their problems only really come to light when Felix has a coronary heart attack. Suddenly they are struck with the chill emptiness of their marriage.

Marriages not infrequently display this slow but progressive drift, not calculated and planned, but as inexorable as if it were part of some deliberate scheme. The partners to such marriages tend to feel that their separate lives in some way will be personally enriching and that their separate and individual development will communicate itself to the relationship. Yet, this has not happened and there has been a gradually increasing detachment and psychological isolation.

Correcting this tendency, perhaps less dramatically marked in most cases than in that of Josephine and Felix, is a prime concern for couples. It is not, as previous points have emphasized, that there is a need for a caring reaction and so on, but that there is a need to keep open a line of communication on personal awareness. Really knowing how your partner *feels*, as opposed to knowing how he or she regards sentencing policy for criminals or the benefits of immunization of babies, is the important area of concern.

Setting aside talking time in a planful way is a means of maintaining this level of contact. Naturally, this will involve th descriptions and discussion of interests, jobs, friends, family problems, and the like, but it must also represent an attempt to look behind these things. Telling how you feel, of your hopes and your fears, is the important message. Self-disclosure is a vital part of these exchanges between you and your partner, each trying to say something about himself or herself, perhaps looking back at one's hopes and desires as a way of informing each other about the changes that have occurred in yourself.

The discussions should take place on a regular basis and room has to be found to hold them. They are not to be regarded as something that can happen when time is left over, but as an essential part of the contract that will keep you together.

SUMMARY OF THE POINTS IN THIS CHAPTER

1. Factors such as illness, ageing, culture and ethnic origin, can affect the stability of marriage. Prospective partners must recognize that long-term relationships need effort to sustain, even when such factors are not present. It is important to ask oneself searching questions about adverse influences and decide whether one has the coping resources to meet such challenges. But some major influences cannot be anticipated and, additionally, the evidence suggests that many couples do not want to recognize their importance.

2. It is generally assumed that marriage will take care of problems and differences whereas, in fact, it often serves to expose them. It is highly important to avoid taking things for granted and becoming complacent about your marriage. Relationships need our constant attention if they are to provide the long-term satisfaction and happiness we hope to gain.

3. Every relationship needs time for the partners involved to have and keep a part of their life for themselves. Marriage does not mean that everything and every moment is to be shared or compromised by your partner's view. Having and feeling that one has a life independent of one's partner increases self-esteem, self-respect, and provides a perspective for us to appreciate what we get from sharing.

4. Every relationship requires that we share, and most of our lives together will be about sharing. Be planful about this, making these aspects of your life open and 'public', not leaving them to chance or whim.

5. Time must be set aside to be especially nice. Don't balk at this being a deliberate and conscious effort but, rather, take pride in the fact that you have thought to do so. Don't leave being nice to those times when you are repaying something your partner has done for you. However, you *can* relish the prospect that 'being nice' produces a similar reaction from your partner.

Showing that you still care

6. Continuing affection is at the heart of lasting relationships. Helping this to happen is aided by keeping alive the romantic attachment; so, don't forget the words, tokens, and behavior that show your partner that you still care.

7. As our relationship continues and passes through its many stages we all will undergo change. See these changes in yourselves in a positive light, not to be resisted or regretted, but as something to be valued. Make use of changes to see new value in each other and as an extension and enrichment of the relationship.

8. Helping days enhance our relationships not simply by relieving the burden of work for our partner, but showing that we are interested and that we care. Make sure that these are planned rather than happen by chance or as an afterthought.

9. We don't marry to change our partners, nor should we, having discovered the warts, insist on their removal. Good relationships involve the mutual recognition of differences and how these enrich a relationship. Where changes are needed to preserve good relations, then they should be made in accordance with the rules set out earlier in this book.

10. Keeping our relationship in good repair is helped by regular discussions about our deeper feeling more than by our superficial interests and needs. It is essential again to find time for these exchanges and not to regard them as something that takes place when all the 'more important' matters have been taken care of.

CHAPTER 8

Avoiding and Dealing with Stress in your Relationship

Harriet and Douglas had managed their relationship quite well. Not that they had made a conscious effort about it, but they were simply not the kind of folk to make a lot of fuss about things and just got on with what they had to do. It wasn't until Douglas became aware that there were lay-offs in this section that he started to worry. At first this was only a fleeting concern over what they'd do about the mortgage if he lost his job but, gradually, this anxiety increased until the threat of redundancy became a reality.

He remembered the day well. It wasn't a shock in one sense – he'd had the foreboding for months earlier – but he recalls looking numbly at the unopened envelope the foreman had passed to him and to several others in the office. He didn't need to open it and just put it into his overalls, his mind a turmoil of apprehension.

From that time on Douglas became more inward-looking, morose, and irritable. Harriet's attempts to get him to look on the bright side seemed to have the opposite effect, if anything, to that intended. He was surly and unresponsive at home and everyone in the house became more quiet and fearful in case he turned his frustration upon them. For Douglas, the loss of his job was not just a blow to his financial standing but a direct attack upon his personal self-esteem and his status in the family. He *could* have handled things differently but, instead, he turned his bitterne against himself and his family, striking out blindly at the wrong that he felt had been done.

Harriet, for her part, put up with Douglas's misery and resentfulness very well for a time but, after a few months, she had had quite enough. After all, she reasoned, lots of people lose their jobs and manage to pick themselves up and go on, but Douglas was becoming just a drag on the family, the attention and support he had got from them seemingly of no help whatsoever.

Norman, on the other hand, was finding his wife's illness a source of stress that made every day an immense effort of coping. Vera had developed multiple sclerosis some years earlier and was now gravely handicapped. Although Norman took as much time as he could from work to look after her and the children, the burden had become heavier to bear as time went on. Vera, too, was now more moody, irritable, and disturbed as the impact of what was happening to her physically became obvious. Norman badly wanted to just cut and run from it all but he knew he couldn't go through with such action and could only brace himself to plod on in what seemed to be an impossible world.

Gavin's job as an export sales manager has become unbearable. A few years back, he recalled, he had greatly enjoyed his work and was really on top of things, but now the company was in deep financial trouble and the Sales Director was at his throat. Gavin had tried everything he knew to boost sales, his efforts taking him away from home a good deal, which he knew Lena hated, but it couldn't be helped. He worked very long hours trying to motivate the sales force to do better, but the more effort he put into the job the more the sales figures seemed to fall. Life at work was a grotesque parody of what it had been, and life at home had become soured and unhappy.

Stresses of one sort or another affect all of us. The problems facing Douglas, Norman, Gavin and their partners may sound exceptional and, certainly, these difficulties call for courage, resourcefulness, and perseverance of an unusual kind. Some, remarkably, seem to be able to rise to meet such challenges and can cope well with adversity; some appear to buckle at the first sign of things going wrong. What is clear, however, is that the ability to handle stresses has a major bearing on the stability of marriage and, in turn, the stability of marriage has importance in helping us to cope with stress.

KEEF

Buckling at the first sign of things going wrong

While our reactions to stress are partly due to our natural temperament and disposition, there *are* things that we can do to increase our resistance to the problems that arise, and some ways in which we can learn to avoid stresses. Douglas could not control the preservation of his job, but he could have controlled the reaction to that loss which made things so much worse. Norman wasn't responsible for Vera's illness, but he could have taken some steps to keep the stresses a little lower; his pride and sense of guilt would not allow him to do so. Gavin couldn't do much about his company's decline, but he could have controlled the effects which this had upon him. Many of us, confronted by stresses, tend to neglect some pretty obvious things that we could do to offset the pressures upon us and feel, instead, that our 'natural' reaction to stress is both understandable and normal. Stresses, whether from within the marriage or outside it, are the enemy of marital adjustment and the control of stress is a major concern for both partners.

While all of us can recognize the big stress when it comes, the smaller ones tend to get overlooked as unimportant. It is not only a good thing to examine these lesser influences, so that we can see how far we can control them, but it is also worth remembering that the building up of many smaller stresses can act in the same way as a single major upset. Tina is a good example of the way this can happen.

Tina has a young family, a part-time job as a secretary, and a husband in advertising. Tom thinks Tina is 'wonderful-at-times' since she seems so very capable of taking care of the kids, so effective as the secretary to an important consultant who 'thinks the world of her', and so marvelous a housewife and social entertainer to the many visitors to their home. But Tom is a bit concerned at the moment since Tina doesn't seem to be coping nearly so well as usual. Mind you, her parents have both had serious illnesses that have upset Tina and she's had to fit in lots of visits to them, cook and clean for them, and so on. Tom thinks she will be fine again when her parents return to good health; then she can go back to looking after the kids, doing her secretarial job, looking after his business associates, taking care of the home and him, and just doing as she always did. Tom has simply never considered how much Tina's life keeps her at full stretch all the time and that there just isn't any more 'give' when some extra problem, however small, arises. He tends to look at each of the separate things that Tina does as really not terribly demanding and doesn't appreciate how they combine into a very considerable personal load.

Sometimes he sees that Tina is really struggling, and he makes a special effort to give her a break by cooking the supper or giving her a 'lie-in' on Sunday morning. His efforts are spasmodic and, in the circumstances, ludicrously small, but he doesn't seem to notice this. Indeed, he goes on blithely in this way until the day when Tina comes to a full stop or becomes ill; at such times Tom feels that she is leaving everything to him, and not that he has allowed her to carry too heavy a burden for too long.

Of course, to place the entire blame on Tom for his lack of insight would be quite wrong. It is true that he has failed to take account of all that Tina does, he had attached unrealistic expectations to her activities, and he has given her his 'good regard' for coming up to scratch so well. He *should* have been more conscious of Tina's load, he *should* have been more realistic and fair about what would be reasonable, and he *should not* have put Tina in the position of earning his good opinion only by managing the impossible. But Tina, for her part, accepted her lot in life, has been active and eager to take on all her commitments, and takes a personal pride in being thought of as 'such a good manager.' Furthermore, she has tended to think of Tom as a poor cook, lousy at disciplining the children, no good at cleaning house, and so on, so there wasn't any point to press him to help out. She has accepted, too, Tom's implicit view that what *he* does is important and what *she* does is to act as a general support to him. 'After all', as he explained later, 'I'm doing this for all of us', to convey the notion that *he* feels equally hard pressed doing a difficult job and doing it without complaint.

KEEPING A TRACK OF STRESS

In the light of what has been said, keeping some kind of check on the stresses and strains we experience is an important exercise. If we know where the stresses are coming from, then we have a chance to do something about them.

Usually, a typical period of two weeks should be enough to provide a useful guide about such matters. Usually, too, a quite simple form of assessment, that you can complete easily, is sufficient for the purpose and should be made on a daily basis. The basic idea is to look at all your main activities, whether brief or lengthy, giving each one a rating for both its unpleasantness and for the length of time that activity has taken.

The stress rating of an activity might be as follows:

1 = An activity that is totally lacking in stress, is enjoyable and relaxing.
2 = An activity involving some degree of stress and strain.
3 = An activity definitely not enjoyable and which involves considerable stress.

This stress value (1,2, or 3) is added to the amount of time the stress lasts, giving 1 for each hour or part of an hour of stress duration.

A visit to the dentist might earn a stress rating of 3 but, since the stress lasts less than one hour, the total is only $3 + 1 = 4$. The drive to work may take $1\frac{1}{2}$ hrs; because of road works and the frustration involved it earns a stress rating of 2, giving $2 + 2 = 4$

as the total strain. Our early morning shower was relaxing, so it has a stress value of 1 and when added to the amount of time ($\frac{1}{2}$ hour) gets a low score $1 + 1 = 2$. An intense stress over a long period clearly earns a high score.

This is only a rough-and-ready assessment but it does help you to understand when the stresses are occurring, what causes them, and where the problem needs to be tackled.

In Tina's case, one can quite easily see any number of possibilities to reduce stress. For example, some chores can be taken over by Tom while others, desirable as they may be, can be seen as inessential and can be dropped altogether.

Other ways could involve Tom and Tina's children doing things for themselves for a change, while Tina can be encouraged to be far less solicitous about them than has been her habit. It usually comes as a pleasant surprise to the stressed individual to see how quite simple and easy-to-achieve steps can make an enormous difference.

Patrick arrives home usually around half-past seven. He's too tired to do anything but slump in his armchair and wait for Yvette to serve him his gin and tonic and his supper. He sees the young children only briefly during the week while, at weekends, he's too busy working on his papers and feels too exhausted to play football in the garden or take the family out.

On the face of it Patrick is an unlucky man who simply happens to have a job that demands too much of him. He's very ready to point out that he can't manage without giving the 100 per cent effort he is currently making and, like Tom, he feels that he is really doing all this for his family. Patrick's wife and children, on the other hand, while appreciating (if they stop to think about it, which they rarely do) the comparative affluence they enjoy, have few satisfactions from having him around. When we look closely at just how he spends his time it is apparent that it is not so much that Patrick is in charge of his job as that the job is in charge of him.

Patrick wants to be everything to everybody, he wants to be liked, to be thought of as an effective and efficient person, to be seen as hard-working and concerned. Indeed, he *is* all these things – except where his family is concerned. They have become the sacrifice that Patrick must make to deal with what he considers to be the priorities in his life.

Broadly speaking, what we think of as stress can be traced to the action of four separate influences. To be aware of the way these forces operate in our own lives is a very good start to gaining control and giving a proper interpretation to our stress diary.

BASIC SENSITIVITY

It will be obvious that we all stand at some point on a line we can call 'sensititivy'. Some of us are 'thick-skinned' and quite impervious to the bumps, knocks, and abrasions that life provides. Some are so tender-minded or thin-skinned that the very smallest upset tips us off balance and we feel anxious and distressed for days. Most of us lie somewhere between these two extremes, but it is useful to see just where we stand so that, if we are at the more sensitive end of the scale, we might be more able to put our feelings of stress and strain into better perspective – by actually **doing** something about our exaggerated sensitivity. Two ways we can use are positive self-talk and learning how to relax.

SELF-TALK

Being aware of having an inclination to react too strongly can of itself help our control. Women with marked tendencies to feel upset pre-menstrually, for example, can help themselves to achieve control by using good 'self-talk.' Some examples of this are:

'I know it's the time of the month . . . just keep calm and don't get too upset.'
'I may say and do things rashly and wrongly . . . just watch it for the next day or two . . .'

In fact most of us use this type of 'internal' talk at some time or another but we don't usually make it a conscious and deliberate form of self-help. If we feel we are a bit sensitive we can learn to use this type of mental mechanism to keep a grip on our reactions to stress. Some examples of the instructions we can employ in talking to ourselves are:
'Don't over-react . . . I know I tend to respond in an exaggerated way, so just keep control.'

'Calmly does it . . . don't let rip, nothing *really* serious has happened.'

'I know I can really handle this problem . . . it's not too big for me to deal with if I don't let my feelings get out of hand.'

'I know I'm OK . . . as good as the next man . . . there's really no need to let this thing get to me . . . just simmer down.'

'If I relax and think about it, nothing very bad has happened . . . I'm just not going to let this thing bowl me over.'

'I'm inclined to take little things too seriously . . . I'm not going to react as if this is a catastrophe, because it isn't . . .'

'This isn't the end of the world . . . just calm down and stop getting too jittery.'

LEARN TO RELAX

Another way of handling excessive sensitivity is to learn how to relax. The best way of doing this is to get your instruction from an expert (usually a clinical psychologist) but there are plenty of self-teaching tapes to be obtained commercially. Some people seem to be able to acquire the skill of relaxing by following quite simple written instructions, however, and an example of this type of self-training is given in Appendix 2 at the end of this book. There are really just two things to remember about this type of therapy. First, the skill of relaxing is gained over a period of time by frequent and regular practice sessions, so be ready to give time to this. Second, the skill acquired in practice sessions is of little value unless the art of relaxing **is applied when it is needed**. So, not only do you regularly carry out your training sessions but you make a point of applying what you have learned to everyday activities, especially those that ordinarily would create tension and stress. Try to keep as relaxed as you can in those situations, compatible with efficient performance.

THE USE OF DRUGS

Medication is sometimes necessary, at least as a temporary measure, to tone down excessive reactions. Understandably, doctors are showing reluctance, these days, to prescribing tranquilizing drugs for long periods of time – or at all, unless the individual's personal circumstances justify it. Only a small proportion of the population are so sensitive that drugs are going to be a necessary part of their rehabilitation, and family doctors will advise on this.

ACTUAL LIFE STRESSES

The kind of things that happened to Douglas and Norman (loss of job and debilitating illness) are readily understood by most of us as important sources of stress. Often only one such stress in our lives is needed to produce abnormal behavior and feelings of distress but, not infrequently, there is a kind of knock-on effect of the main stress that makes everything considerably worse. When Douglas loses his job, his resulting morose attitude and sullen behavior begin to affect his family who, in turn, find themselves unable to be as loving and supporting as they would wish to be. When Norman is faced with the immense physical and psychological effort involved in looking after Vera, sheer fatigue sometimes makes him react in a tetchy way to quite reasonable requests that Vera may make; Vera reacts badly since her feelings of guilt and dependence combine with the sheer misery of being helpless, and so they add to their problems by shouting things that will make them feel even worse.

Fortunately, most of our stresses have only temporary effects and many will be rather easier to tackle than those affecting Douglas and Norman. To look at the stresses that one is facing is a considerable help and is a first step toward dealing with them. Your actual stress score can be assessed using the questionnaire in Appendix 1. Suggestions about the ways in which stresses should be tackled are included later in this chapter.

COPING ABILITIES

Most people, through experience, have acquired basic coping abilities. We have learned to control the instant rage that frustration can produce in the young child, we have the capacity to postpone satisfactions, we have developed an aptitude for reasoning with others with whom we disagree, and so on. But, sometimes such abilities have been lost or never properly acquired, and we need to review our standing on those skills too. In effect, assessing our ability to cope is another way of evaluating our strengths and weaknesses in respect of dealing with stress, and a check on this can be made by calculating the score on the relevant part of the questionnaire in Appendix 1.

You will notice that one of the questions refers to the asset of having support from others, rather than to a personal attribute. Really this is not a personal coping skill (or lack of it) but it is included in the Coping Scale simply because such support adds to our own capacity to deal with stress.

PERSONALITY TYPE

There is a good deal of evidence that stress is often self-imposed. Some people, for example, drive themselves hard, are achievement oriented, and find themselves unable to take a relaxed view of life. For such people the ordinary bumps, bruises, and frustrations of life are obstacles to be overcome and challenges to be continually met. Those successful in their working lives often have this temperament which, when controlled, can be a great asset but when displayed in every facet of life can be stress-producing.

John, aged 18, dolefully recalled that his father, a highly successful businessman, never allowed him to do anything without constant interference, frequently taking over the job because John wasn't doing it quite well enough. Rodney is perpetually telling June how to manage the house – he simply can't understand how she can be so inefficient. Jean can't even play a game of table tennis with the kids without beating them, never giving them the opportunity of a 'success' experience. Sadie is regarded by most people at the amateur dramatics society as altogether too pushy and perfectionistic – it simply stops being fun when she's involved. Gordon is dreaded by his neighbors because he doesn't allow them to do their own home repairs; he's good, they admit, but he wants them to do the job *his* way. At work, Justin can't delegate to any subordinate without worrying about the way it's done; he's constantly checking on his staff and, quite frequently, does the job all over again after hours because he's not happy about it. Harry, too, belongs to this group; he's irritated by the incredibly slow rate (to him) of work by others, he works so fast that he is actually given a lot more to do.

These characteristics, in some ways desirable, actually place stress on the individuals in whom they are found – and in those with whom they interact.' In moderation, they are advantageous and useful but, to excess, they are often a handicap. The Stress Prone Personality measure in the questionnaire is your score on these qualities.

When you have completed the questionnaire, check your scores on all the four influences to obtain your stress profile, using the key to each question in Appendix 1 **only after you have given your answers**. Simply add up the number of Personal Sensitivity items, Actual Life Stresses, Coping Abilities, and Stress Prone Personality items to arrive at four total scores, then check your totals against those for the average person. Much higher scores than the average will be your pointer to taking action on any one of these totals and the kind of things you might try are described in the next section.

SOME OF THE THINGS TO DO ABOUT STRESS

SMALL BUT SIGNIFICANT CHANGES

Getting down to doing something about the stresses and strains in our lives is not a matter of making radical and dramatic changes. Rather, it is a question of making some small but definite alterations. Josie's feeling of strain about entertaining her husband's parents every weekend, which leaves her feeling that she never has any time for what *she* wants to do, is not dealt with by refusing to have them at all, but by making a plan to space our their visits. Frank's unwillingness to delegate is not dealt with by giving up all work, but by planned delegation and, having allocated such duties, letting people get on with it. Murray's solution to being a workaholic is not to give up work altogether but to make a conscious effort to separate work from other types of activity. Achieving a balanced approach to life's problems, not feeling one has to do everything or do nothing at all, is what stress reduction is about, keeping in mind that this will have a healthy bearing on our relationships and enhance our lives together.

PICKING YOUR TARGET

Many people, in the middle of a stressful period in their lives, become paralyzed by the sheer number of things that are going wrong. Contemplating the scene of multiple pile-up, they retreat into inactivity and depression and hope that, somehow, it will all sort itself out. Sometimes problems *do* simply melt away but, more often, they grow bigger and more insistent when neglected. The way to deal with the feelings of inertia is to list the problems, select the one that is both important and easy to deal with, and get it under control. Repeat this as many time as necessary.

Sandra selected the problem of caring for her mother who lived alone, was very handicapped by arthritis, and was really a demanding personality. Her way of coping had been simply to do everything herself, running between schools, her own home, her mother's home, and her part-time job, cramming everything into the little time available. Not surprisingly, she had become irritable, tired, and depressed by her burdens, and this showed in her relationship with her husband and children. But it wasn't until a crisis occurred that Sandra would admit she simply couldn't cope with all that she had undertaken. Sitting down to talk the problem over with Adam, Sandra began to realize that much of the difficulty stemmed from her unwillingness to ask for help and involve the rest of the family. Indeed, she was surprised by the way Adam and the children responded to the plan they formed which allowed the kids to help out with visits to Sandra's mother, Adam to get home a few minutes earlier to help with meals, and other ways in which her burden could be made lighter.

Instead of just allowing problems to build up, our aim should be to examine them and look at possible solutions. Not every problem will have an easy answer, but at least we can take a look at what is going on and what alternatives *are* open to us. When you have solved this problem – or decided there is absolutely nothing you can do about it, however small – then go on to look at the next one on your list.

BEING EVERYTHING TO EVERYBODY

In part, Sandra's problem is that she wants to be a good daughter, a good wife, a good mother, a good part-time librarian, a good cook, and so on. She wants to be everything to everybody and really hasn't got down to the job of selecting what is *really* important to do, and cutting out the less essential. The list of stresses and strains that you make should be divided into things that really matter and things that can be put off or dropped ltogether.

Dominic is a busy accountant and works long hours. He is a concerned and active man outside business hours, too, and belongs to a number of organizations with charitable aims. This takes up nearly all of his 'spare' time and his wife and family complain that he never has time for them. Dominic feels at full stretch, but he doesn't know quite what to do about pleasing his family and going on with all the work he has taken on. His aim must be to make some cuts, but he has never been able to bring himself to do this; rather, he has been only too willing to take on more work and, like all willing horses, he has been given a very heavy load.

Dominic isn't being asked to give up all charitable work, nor is he being asked to make an unreasonable sacrifice. What he is required to do is to examine his commitments and to arrive at a more reasonable balance, so that he can give the care and attention to his relationship that is needed. He must sit down with his family to consider the way he allocates his time and, with them, arrive at a more appropriate plan.

BEING AT THE MERCY OF THE ENVIRONMENT

Carl built up his business from scratch. He still runs the (now international) company from home, taking calls from Singapore and elsewhere in the middle of the night. How, he wonders, could one possibly do anything about this, since the calls *are* important to his business and there isn't anyone else to take them. Carl has never actually sat down to examine the situation effectively; the 24-hour phone service he runs as a one-man band is something he has come to regard as the natural and inescapable result of being successful.

Beatrice is a 'soft touch' for people with problems. It is true that she is not only a very sympathetic and warm person, but she is also full of good advice. No wonder the world of problems frequently finds its way to her door. In fact, Beatrice hardly has any time to get through the things *she* wants to do because she is so busy sorting out other people's difficulties. She likes to be helpful and we can recognize that she is very good at being so, but she simply doesn't know how to turn off the tap.

Being available to all the world at all times is simply not compatible with leading an unstressed existence. Again, priorities have to be made clear – just what it is that you **must** do – and which surplus commitments can be jettisoned, however hard this may seem at first sight.

LEARNING TO SAY 'NO'

Saying 'yes' can become simply a bad habit. Maybe the word itself isn't always used, but the generally compliant attitude and behavior is too much in evidence. Saying 'yes' does produce good feelings in others and may mean that you are held in high regard but, quite often, it simply spells exploitation and taking the 'yes' person for granted. Some people have become afraid of saying 'no', either because they feel they will lose the good will of others or cause upset, but it is important to realize that, properly applied, a 'no' gains the respect of others and is often the start to solving problems.

Philip is a 'good guy.' He is the head of his section at work and is always ready to help out when any of his junior staff have a problem. He's always willing, too, when senior management asked his section to take on extra work and has never turned down any request of this kind, even though he has to do most of the extra work himself as the only highly skilled man in the section. Philip doesn't know that, by saying 'no', he can get his boss to appreciate that there are not enough skilled people in the section and that the work could be carried out more effectively if new people could be brought in.

The way Philip finally dealt with the matter was not simply to say 'no' but to point out to his boss that the extra work would require re-scheduling of existing jobs, and that he would be happy to fit in the new work on whatever priority was given to it. To Philip's astonishment his boss decided that more personnel *were* needed to help in the section.

'I HAVE TO . . .

Related to the foregoing is the 'I have to' habit. Many of us have a tendency to say 'I have to' do this or that without questioning at all whether it *is* essential and a 'must.' Taking away the stress and strain of life is often helped by looking at our 'have-to's' and asking, perhaps for the first time, whether it really is so. Our tendency, when we first pull ourselves up short with such a question, will be to decide 'Yes, I really do have to . . .', but we should go on to ask ourselves about the consequences of *not doing* the thing. Most frequently the answer to the question will be that there are no serious consequences at all – we have simply got into the habit of saying this or that *must* be done.

Joan felt that she had to always give Gerry a 'good hot meal' every night and spent a great deal of time in preparation and thought about what variety she could introduce on each occasion. She had overlooked the fact that Gerry didn't actually always want a 'good hot meal' when he got home and would often have been happy with a snack. Joan puts an unnecessary strain on her personal resources by 'having to' do something that really isn't needed at all.

SETTING OUT TO WIN

The need to win has been mentioned in earlier chapters as something to be avoided in conflict situations, decision-making, and other contexts. Some people, as has been pointed out in this chapter, have an overdeveloped need to win and find it difficult to play a game of cards without getting angry with a partner for doing the wrong thing, or playing table tennis with the kids in a relaxed way, or having a game of golf without wanting to smash the clubs when they slice the ball. Winning is important in the right context, but some people clearly find it hard to distinguish between when this is a real advantage and when the need to win has become a handicap to enjoyment and a bore to others. Just as important, from the point of view of stress, is that the mobilizing of personal resources to make sure one wins, and the failure to enjoy what might otherwise be a pleasant form of relaxation, can actually be harmful to oneself. Setting out to win all the time is a wearing and stress-inducing habit that has to be eliminated.

Insight, gained simply by looking at what one does, is the most useful start to identifying the fault. Most individuals guilty of this type of habit already know about it but tend to say, 'well, that's just the way I am', or to justify it in some other way, for example, by saying that the children must be taught to compete as a preparation for life. There is, in short, a reluctance to change

Nevertheless, the stressed individual must examine thi

aspect of behavior and see to what extent he or she can make a real effort to become more relaxed when winning really doesn't matter.

DELEGATION

The willingness to delegate – or lack of it – has already appeared in some of the case examples given. Sandra had to learn that her family could help out, if asked; Carl feels he really should go on being a one-man band; and Philip is always too eager to take on someone else's work. Some people strongly dislike delegation since they feel no one can do the job quite so competently or as quickly as they themselves, and an example is found earlier in this chapter where a father rarely gave his son a real chance to learn, for these reasons. Answers to particular questions in the Stress Questionnaire in Appendix 1 are also indicative of this tendency, such as 'I prefer to assume complete responsibility rather than share it with others', 'I take pride in getting the job done faster than most', 'I do not suffer fools gladly', and 'I get impatient and angry with incompetence and inefficiency.'

Usually people can appreciate the presence of such characteristics in themselves and the real problem is in recognizing these qualities as possible faults. For the most part the individual unwilling to delegate takes the view that it is entirely reasonable to behave as he or she does, and finds it hard to become more relaxed about things. Being aware of the need to change, to recognize that there are other views than one's own, and to accord some role to the less competent, are matters to which attention should be paid. Again, it is not a root-and-branch change that is being called for, but simply a little more 'give' on the part of those reluctant to delegate. The gain, of course, is a reduction of the stresses and strains on those same individuals.

SET APPROPRIATE TIME SCHEDULES

Stressed people spend a good deal of time rushing around in frenetic activity but not necessarily getting much done. They justify this activity by saying there is too much to do and too little time available and, sometimes, they are right. Bad planning, failure to delegate effectively, saying 'I have to', and so on, may indeed mean that there is no alternative but to do everything at a gallop.

Although at first it may sound an odd way of dealing with the problem, the most sensible thing is to actually slow down the rate of activity. This allows one to be much more deliberate and considered in the things that are done and leaves less room for making mistakes. By and large, efficiency is increased rather than decreased by adopting a measured (*not* very slow) pace.

PLAN TO AVOID STRESS

Stress avoidance involves planning for a balanced existence, making sure that one or another area of life does not get an unfair allocation of time. Leisure pursuits, for example, should not be seen as the things one does when everything important has been achieved; leisure and relaxation are themselves important and are not simply to be fitted into left-over space. Don't allow leisure time to be available or not, according to how busy you are, but *plan* for leisure as a vital aspect of stress avoidance.

In fact life planning needs careful consideration so that appropriate schedules can be set for family, work, personal interests, social activities, and leisure pursuits. The time each occupies will depend on individual taste, and preference, but work – or personal interests – should not be allowed to erode time allocated to our partners.

Roy's life is his work. For him there is little else and, while professing a good deal of affection for his family, he rarely has an opportunity for showing it directly.

Joe's main interest is golf. He is very fond of Maisie but, so far as he is concerned, they should be together on the golf course, together in the club house, together watching the golf international, and so on.

Both Roy and Joe allow a personal interest to exert an overwhelming influence on their marriages and, while they themselves would not concede the point, they are demanding that their marriages fit into this unbalanced pattern. The way in which the allocation of time is made is a matter for *both* partners to decide. A satisfactory plan – even if it is not one that either partner would most prefer – is one that they can both agree to

CURBING AGGRESSION

Conflict and aggressive behavior have been discussed in a previous chapter, when it was pointed out that anger narrows one's view of things and tends to produce similar reactions in others. Some people, because of the stress and frustrations that life brings, have tended to adopt a more assertive and autocratic style in general, developing the habit of responding impulsively and waspishly to the mildest provocation.

Personal anger is a stress, and the more it is controlled the less strain the individual will suffer. A review of your week should be enough to tell you whether you are guilty of allowing angry emotion too big a place in your life. Ask yourself whether you have sounded the car horn too much, shouted too often at the kids, cussed too often, slammed doors, etc. Ask yourself if these actions helped you in any way to deal with what happened. Did those at whom you hooted behave well as a result, or did they make offensive gestures? Did the kids become better because you shouted? Did swearing unjam the lock? Or, did you wind yourself up to no good purpose? Set yourself the task next week of trying to play things low key. Deliberately show tact and consciously express humor. Make a special effort to see the other point of view. Try not to get uptight about the things that go wrong – they'll probably go wrong just as often but, by keeping your reactions under control, you can spare yourself stress and strain.

SLOWING DOWN

Some people live at 100 miles per hour, as if life itself depended on the sheer speed of doing things. Frenzied application to everything is seen as a sign of virtue by the one doing the rushing around, proving to the world that he or she can't be accused of laziness. Sometimes such individuals come to feel that any kind of quiet contemplation or leisure pursuit is 'suspect' and they feel obliged to find 'something useful to do' to fill all their waking hours.

It hardly needs to be said that such people impose considerable strains upon themselves as well as making everyone else feel comfortable. Slowing down, taking things a little easier, and having time to stop and reflect, are all desirable objectives. There shouldn't be the slightest twinge of guilt, for example, if a little time is spent on such 'unconstructive' occupations as leaning on a fence, looking at the stained-glass windows in a cathedral, or just admiring the view. This is not really wasted time at all, but time very well spent by providing essential rest pauses in a busy day and a valuable perspective on life generally.

A life simply packed with chores, excluding reflection, tradition, ceremony, and plain 'time wasting' is not only narrow and restricting but actually imposes stresses that can be seen in our relationships with others. Effort must be made to program time more effectively so that short rest pauses are built into our day; this will help us to avoid feelings of exhaustion and increase our efficiency, rather than reduce it. A few suggestions along these lines are:

1. Take clear lunch breaks – don't just snatch a sandwich while still working. Make the effort to actually sit down, eat in a deliberately relaxed and unhurried way. Turn your mind to pleasant topics that have nothing to do with work. Try to spend at least half an hour on this type of break in your day.

2. Space out your daily work, taking brief (say, 5 minute) rest pauses in the middle of the morning and afternoon. Either try to get yourself completely relaxed, physically, or do something enjoyable and completely different during these breaks. There is something wrong with your work organization if you cannot find the necessary ten minutes in your day.

3. Try to set realistic life goals and ambitions. Set out to examine, in a detailed way, just what you are doing and why. Ask yourself whether the pace at which you are now living is really important to you. Ask whether the deadlines that fill your life are really necessary or if you have simply come to believe that they are.

4. Be tidy! We all tend to react to the general appearance of the world and, if it seems disorderly and chaotic, we can find ourselves reacting in like manner. There is no need to be scrupulously tidy, but simply avoid letting things get really out of hand.

5. Try getting up just a few minutes earlier each day (it really isn't impossible) to simply potter around, allowing yourself to wake up gradually. Don't leave only just enough time to

things, and then find you have to rush around to get everything ready – once you start to rush it can be hard to stop.
6. Avoid all 'speed-up' activities. Check yourself. Do you walk
   too quickly, talk too rapidly, hurry the speech of others and
   finish their sentences for them? Do you rush your reading and
   are you in the habit of doing two things at once? Do you tend
   to butt into conversations too much and do you tend to try to
   turn the topic to what *you* want to talk about? Do you only
   pretend to listen when others are making their point so that
   you can think of the next thing that *you* are going to say?

A SIMPLE ANTI-STRESS PACKAGE

While all the rules given are important, and some attempt should
be made to put them into practice to deal with your personal
stress, there are a few further simple rules that should always be
kept in mind.

1. Try to stay calm. You may not always make it, but try to cut out
   surplus and needless anger reactions.
2. Keep things in perspective. Don't jump to conclusions and
   react impulsively; reflect and discuss more often.
3. Use relaxation and make room in your life for leisure activities.
4. Share problems with others. Don't become a bore – but you *are*
   entitled to support and empathy from people close to you.

SUMMARY OF POINTS IN THIS CHAPTER

Life stresses are the enemy of personal relationships: the more we
control them the better partner we will become. While we cannot
do a great deal about our personal sensitivity, it is possible to
avoid unnecessary stress or reduce its impact on us.

1. Good communication is essential to avoid interpersonal
   stress. Don't just put up with an unacceptable role until it
   becomes impossible – discuss with your partner and come to
   a sensible arrangement.
2. Keep a running check on stresses in your life. Even the
   smaller ones, when added together, can become an excessive
   burden.

3. Positive self-talk can help us to keep the stresses and strains in our lives in better proportion.

4. Learn to relax. When life's problems loom large, our bodily tension increases. Counteract this tendency.

5. Don't try too hard to solve all your problems and expect to finally eliminate all trace of them. That usually isn't possible. Rather, concentrate on *reducing* stress: even a small reduction in each stress can mean a big difference in our ability to cope.

6. Don't try to be everything to everybody all the time. Take a sensible view of your commitments and see what you can *reasonably* do – then do that.

7. Don't be at the mercy of your environment. You really *can* re-arrange your world to fit in with what you want to happen.

8. Learn to say 'no.' Don't feel that you have to accept whatever is given to you. Examine the reasonableness of what is dished out and feel free to say 'no' sometimes.

9. Cut down on the 'have to.' Question what you tend to take for granted, don't just go ahead and do it because you have always done so.

10. Don't set out to win everything. When it really doesn't matter, then just try taking a more relaxed approach.

11. Delegate. Whether at work or at home, don't always feel that it must be *your* job and don't go along with the idea that no one else could do it quite as well. Spread the load more.

12. Slow down. Don't set impossible schedules for yourself, and deliberately introduce rest pauses into your day.

13. Get balance into your life. Find time for leisure, hobbies, the family, social life, and yourself as well as for work.

14. Curb aggression. Plan your way through problems – you'll end up feeling much better.

15. Check out your scores on the Stress Questionnaire (p. 167) and see where improvements can be made.

CHAPTER 9

Behavior and Change

The notion of an ideal union, of a destiny bringing together one man and one woman in perfect harmony is, sadly, a romantic illusion. Not that romance is a bad thing or that loving relationships are pure fiction, but the idea of soulmates for whom a kindly fate intended each other is mistaken. In fact, to think of relationships in purely romantic terms can be dangerous: many of our moments together will not fall into this category of experience and, if romance is the only asset we bring to our relationship, then the outlook will be gloomy and the outcome a bitter disappointment. The good marriages that we enjoy have been worked for and earned, not the free gift of a kindly fate, while the failing relationship arises largely from our own mistakes. Although serious and unexpected bolts from the blue can upset our partnerships, most of what makes them succeed or fail is actually under our own control. The problems that produce breakdown are rarely the result of some malignant influence outside ourselves but are, overwhelmingly, the price we pay for our own unwillingness or inability to deal with them in an effective way. So we see that the problems encountered in surviving and failing marriages are not unusual but, rather, that they are looked at differently and dealt with differently by the two groups.

Despite the high divorce rates described at the beginning of this book, marriage remains the most popular of voluntary insti-utions, with well over 90 per cent consenting to that state.

Perhaps our idealism and unrealistic expectations of what marriage will bring to us is partly responsible for the fact that so many will quickly want to break the bonds taken on so willingly. But, for most people who seek divorce or separation, 'bad luck' or the 'impossibility of the other person' will be blamed. Only a small number will feel that they entertained unrealistic notions, or were too idealistic, or will be willing to concede that their own faults and fallibilities played a part in the breakdown. For some, the problems of sharing in a balanced and mutually agreed way have become too great. While appearing to be a trivial matter, some 90 per cent of couples report that household chores – and who does what – had become a major area of disagreement. Although it is understandable that problems arise when both partners may be working and come home too tired to face the cleaning and cooking, it is saddening when accusations that one or other partner is failing to do a fair share have so easily displaced more appropriate ways of settling disputes. For others, family ties have become a focus of discord, and a proper balance between obligations to parents and to each other has not been achieved. Keeping parents sweet, while delicately balancing this with personal needs and interests, can be difficult, but the problem is not eased by getting entangled in family disputes, nor by hanging on to parents and remaining dependent on them.

Yet others find that disillusion comes in the middle years of marriage with a growing realization that there has been a steady drift toward taking each other for granted. Gone are the surprise gifts, the lingering glances, and the long, earnest and loving talks, leaving an unfilled void. The nurturing and education of children has often distracted the couple from a consideration of themselves and their relationship, and only when the children are moving on does the neglect of the marriage come to light. Alternatively, the problem may stem from the subordination of one partner's interests to those of the other, often in the form of a wife's acceptance of a supporting role to her husband's career. In all these cases difficulties have arisen from the failure to secure an adequate *balance between competing demands* in which, while we give as much as we can to needs that arise, time is always found for keeping the relationship fresh and growing strongly.

Whatever the reasons for discord and disharmony, in the large majority of cases it is in the interests of the individuals concerned to solve their problems and resolve to stay together. This book has attempted to set out a strategy for achieving this objective, beginning with a contract between partners to make the much needed changes and developing through to the means by which changes can be made to many aspects of interaction. The argument, throughout, is that the couple must not wait for a revival of love and good feeling but, rather, to ensure that the changes in behavior take place *in order* to gain love and respect. This is the only feasible approach where disagreement and hostility have eroded the good feelings that once were there. Understandably, this approach creates one or two problems, the greatest of which is that of overcoming unwillingness to change. Where one or both partners have been gravely hurt, where there is an overwhelming sense of being wronged, and where one or both are asking for something that can't be given, an end to the marriage seems inevitable. However painful the break-up, the prospect of staying together appears out of the question – nothing can be done to ease the hurt, to right the wrong, or to change the other person. Yet, out of this 'terminal' situation the couple have to discover those inner resources that will enable them to keep going and to make a last effort to overcome apparently insuperable obstacles.

In the author's experience, although great doubts about the future may exist, and in spite of immense difficulties, couples usually *are* willing to consider the possibility of looking again at their marriage if there is a faint hope of success and **a realistic plan** for getting it right. Certainly, without some new and workable means of tackling their problems the couple have little chance of success since, very clearly, the old ways have not helped. The behavioral approach outlined here, too, can begin to restore hope because the changes made by each partner are themselves rewarding and, in turn, encourage more changes and even greater hope. Courage and commitment are needed to undertake the task, but the steps themselves are not really difficult and, with some exceptions, once taken can quite quickly lead to a better understanding.

A second major difficulty soon shows itself during the operation of the program, when things are not working out in quite the way that has been agreed between the partners. To some people this is taken as a sign of the lack of cooperation and commitment that has been feared and more than half expected, leading to the conclusion that it proves the sheer impossibility of the exercise. These disappointments can be the last straws that lead to pressing the abort button on the whole program.

It is not easy for the individual who feels that, once again, his or her efforts have been in vain, to accept that even the best of plans will not always work smoothly. Things *will* go wrong, mistakes *will* be made, misunderstandings *will* happen and, sometimes, one partner *will* want to test out the relationship like a child finding out how far it can try the patience of a parent. To expect progress without a hitch is wildly optimistic; the bad patches must be anticipated and worked through, and have to be seen as the spur to new effort and understanding rather than as a cause for despair. The couple must keep their eyes fixed on the main target of building a better relationship and realize that, in this way, they are serving their own interests as well as those of others. Staying together makes a lot of sense for both partners and their dependants.

Observing the rules set out in this book does not guarantee success – some relationships are going to fail despite the strenuous efforts of partners. Yet, following the rules will greatly increase the chances of marriage survival and, with a bit of determined application, many people are surprised by the extent of the changes that can be made. One of the rewards that frequently occurs is the discovery that a confident prediction about a partner's faults is disproved – the old, familiar way of behaving, that caused so much distress, no longer appears. The change may involve only small parts of behavior but can make all the difference to our view of the future.

To begin with, progress tends to be marked by caution and only tentative steps toward change, neither partner wanting to give too much, to lose ground, or to take trust too far. Step by step the couple may be discovering that the old labels and expectations are being demolished and have to be discarded. But habits and views built up during more troubled times will die hard, and a sensitivity to things going wrong will stay around for some time. This is only an intermediate stage and, as more advances and changes take place, the relationship improves and the couple can experience feelings that have been dormant for a long time. It is important not to be impatient when progress is slow, but som find it very difficult to be restrained and to avoid trying to hurry things along to the next stage. The man who only last week entered a contract to save his marriage is expecting too much if, this week, he wants his wife to display the warm affection of ten years ago. A willingness to work patiently toward further change and improvement is the rule, seeing each small step as an important contribution to more fundamental and longed-for changes to come.

On occasions a specific problem arises that might require outside and expert help to resolve. For example, the treatment of a specific sexual difficulty, the management of a child with problem behavior, or the care of an elderly and dependent relative, may benefit from outside help when the couple themselves lack the skill and resources to deal with the worry. It is crucial that these difficulties should not be allowed to divide the partners but, rather, are seen as a stress that both must face up to and deal with in a united and supportive way, perhaps making the kind of agreement outlined earlier in this book. It will be noticed, however, that many specific problems of the type mentioned have been the cause of – or at least have been made worse by – an existing poor relationship. Where the couple have made headway with improvements to their relationship, it will be found that the specific stresses and strains that the world brings to them are dealt with much more easily.

Not all of what has been described in this book will be needed by every couple. Where relationships have entered their terminal stages, all aspects of interaction will have been affected and only a determined effort to use every bit of help available will be enough. For others, however, the problem may be the lesser one of marital drift – a gradual deterioration in the quality of the relationship – and the task for the couple will be to become more aware of what has happened and to make use of the relevant rules described. On the other hand, it may be that attention to good communication, or to developing a method of reaching decisions without major disagreement, will be all that is needed. Alternatively, perhaps a means of effectively handling conflicts that tend to erupt too easily and too violently, or simply discovering ways in which a relationship can be enhanced, will be called for. Certainly, there is no requirement to follow all the rules described in every case; in fact, it is perfectly reasonable to take parts of the program or sets of rules, rather than the whole. However, as awareness about where and how problems arise is increased by looking at the whole relationship, it is recommended that couples should read the entire book. The Rules are in the form of a set of interlocking pieces, so reading the whole will not be a redundant exercise. In any case, working with couples dispels the myth that we are all born fully equipped with the skills to make marriage work. Learning to deal with the problems of relationships in a changing world is a task that all of us must face.

OTHER USEFUL READING

Bach, C.R., and Wyden, P. 1974. *The Intimate Enemy: How to Fight Fears in Love and Marriage*. New York: Nash Publ. Co.

Dicks, H.V. 1967. *Marital Tension*. London: Routledge and Kegan Paul

Guerney, B.G., Jr. (Ed.). 1977. *Relationship Enhancement*. San Francisco: Josey-Bass.

Mace, D., and Mace, V. 1974. *We Can Have Better Marriages*. Nashville: Abingdon.

Mace, D. 1983. *Prevention in Family Services: Approaches to Family Wellness*. Beverley Hills: Sage Publ.

Mattison, J., and Sinclair, I. 1979. *Male and Stalemate*. Oxford: Blackwell.

Raush, H.L., Barry, W.A., Hertel, R.K., and Swain, M.A. 1974. *Communication, Conflict and Marriage*. San Francisco: Josey-Bass.

Rowan, J. 1983. *The Reality Game*. London: Routledge and Kegan Paul.

Tyndall, N. 1983. *Marriage Guidance Counselling*. National Marriage Council, UK.

Weiss, R.L. 1975. *Marital Separation*. New York: Basic Books, Inc.

APPENDIX 1

Measuring your Stress Reactions

INSTRUCTIONS

The questionnaire appears on the following pages. Look at each question in turn and answer it, trying not to skip any question. For each question ask yourself whether it describes you or how you feel. If your answer is 'yes', then put a circle around the 'yes', and if 'no', circle the 'no'. On some questions you may find it hard to give a definite 'yes' or 'no' answer, but try to opt for one or the other as the nearest you can get to describing yourself.

Don't seek any other person's help or opinion about how you should answer and don't check out the answers before you have completed the questionnaire.

The method of scoring and what these scores mean is described at the end of the questionnaire.

Remember, you are asking on each question 'Is this like me, is this how I am?'

THE STRESS QUESTIONNAIRE

1. I can take a measured look at a job to be done without feeling an urge to rush into action before getting the thing properly thought out. YES NO

2. I have recently had to give up an important personal relationship. YES NO

3. I often have to find people who will talk me out of my 'blues' YES NO

4. I can control my temper: when I lose it, this is calculated and I don't go beyond what I intended to say or do. YES NO

5. I find it easy to get along with and accept people who hold different points of view to my own. YES NO

6. I tend to find that my mood is very changeable YES NO

7. Having to tolerate delays of any kind is very irritating to me. YES NO

8. I prefer to assume complete responsibility rather than share it with others. YES NO

9. Recent events in my life have forced an important change in my social relationships. YES NO

10. I do not suffer fools gladly. YES NO

11. I can focus on one thing when necessary and clear my mind of other things to be done. YES NO

12. I take pride in getting a job done faster than most other people. YES NO

13. I sometimes feel rather upset without there being anything that has happened to cause this feeling. YES NO

14. I am inclined to be too sensitive to criticism or unkind comment. YES NO

15. Deadlines are very important to me. YES NO

16. I can say 'no' to people who make unreasonable demands without them getting too upset.   YES   NO

17. My sexual needs are largely unsatisfied.   YES   NO

18. I usually try to deal with problems in an organized and systematic way.   YES   NO

19. I have plenty of battles on my hands at work.   YES   NO

20. I have suffered considerably from constant arguments at home or at work.   YES   NO

21. I have very real financial problems.   YES   NO

22. I quite often get a kind of guilty feeling for no good reason.   YES   NO

23. I can get over disappointments without getting too upset, recognizing that one can't have everything the way one wishes.   YES   NO

24. I often feel very 'strung up' and agitated.   YES   NO

25. I can immerse myself in constructive activity as a way of taking my mind away from a problem.   YES   NO

26. I have recently had serious problems in a close relationship.   YES   NO

27. I can usually get other people to see all sides of a problem.   YES   NO

28. I can unwind quickly on holiday and begin to enjoy myself from the start.   YES   NO

29. I enjoy competing at work and elsewhere.   YES   NO

30. I feel I am as good as the next man (or woman).   YES   NO

31. When confronted with a problem I usually remain optimistic about the outcome.   YES   NO

32. I get impatient and angry with incompetence and inefficiency.   YES   NO

33. From time to time I get to feeling upset, shaky, and sweating.   YES   NO

34. I work long hours from choice.   YES   NO

35. I, or members of my family, have recently experienced problems due to illness. YES NO

36. I get irritable and bad-tempered rather too easily. YES NO

37. I drive myself harder than most. YES NO

38. I can usually break down a problem into manageable chunks. YES NO

39. I am a worrier and tend to look on the black side of things. YES NO

40. I have a tendency to go over past problems and brood about what has happened. YES NO

41. I can count on the support of my family and friends. YES NO

42. I have to spend too much time away from home. YES NO

43. I am very ambitious. YES NO

44. I get too jittery when something goes wrong. YES NO

45. I sometimes have to assume responsibility for events over which I have no control. YES NO

46. I tend to put myself down too much and compare myself unfavorably with other people. YES NO

47. Someone close to me has recently died. YES NO

48. At times I have more work to do than I can cope with. YES NO

49. I am able to tell other people what I feel and think; I don't simmer privately or explode. YES NO

50. I tend to get involved in many different ideas and projects. YES NO

51. I don't sleep too well and seem to feel more tired than others. YES NO

52. I have to work and deal with others who have unpredictable and uncertain temperament. YES NO

53. I feel dissatisfied at work due to things like blocked promotion, threat of redundancy, and excessive demands by superiors, etc. YES NO

KEY TO THE STRESS QUESTIONNAIRE

Coping ability
The score here is an indication of how well you have learned to deal in a reasonable way with the ordinary difficulties of life. Obtain the score by counting the number of times you have circled 'no' as your answer to the following questions:

1, 4, 5, 11, 16, 18, 23, 25, 27, 28, 30, 31, 38, 41, 49.

Actual life stresses
The score here is an indication of how many important stresses are acting on your life to upset your adjustment. Obtain the score by counting the number of times you have circled 'yes' as your answer to the following questions:

2, 9, 17, 20, 21, 26, 35, 42, 45, 47, 48, 52, 53.

Stress prone personality
The score here is an indication of your tendency to behave in a way that will impose stresses upon yourself. The score is obtained by counting the number of times you have circled 'yes' as your answer to the following questions:

7, 8, 10, 12, 15, 19, 29, 32, 34, 37, 43, 50.

Personal sensitivity
The score here is a reflection of your tendency to be vulnerable, over-sensitive, take things too seriously and too much to heart. The score is obtained by counting the number of times you have circled 'yes' as your answer to the following questions:

3, 6, 13, 14, 22, 24, 33, 36, 39, 40, 44, 46, 51.

CHECKING THE NORMALITY OF YOUR SCORE

	NORMAL RANGE	STRESS PROBLEM RANGE
Coping ability score (number of 'no' answers)	0 to 5	6 to 15
Actual life stresses score (number of 'yes' answers)	0 to 5	6 to 13
Stress prone personality (number of 'yes' answers)	0 to 5	6 to 12
Personal sensitivity score (number of 'yes' answers)	0 to 6	7 to 13

In each case, the higher the score the greater the degree of difficulty in that area.

APPENDIX 2

A Simple Way of Learning How to Relax

Relaxation training will help you to cope with stress. Using relaxation in demanding and difficult situations stops us from over-reacting and adds greatly to our self-confidence because we can remain in control of the situation. Using relaxation, we can meet the problems of life in a more measured and effective way, and this is of particular importance in our married relationships. Learning to relax takes a little time and effort but practice can soon achieve a useful level of skill. The following brief method is easy to follow and can make an appreciable difference to the self-control we display.

Find a comfortable reclining chair, or lie on your bed, to do these exercises. Choose a time when you can be undisturbed and free from interruptions for about twenty minutes.

The exercises all involve the following general steps:

1. Lightly tense a given group of muscles (as listed below) and hold this tension for a slow count of 5 while holding your breath.
2. During (1) above, focus your attention on the sensations in the part of your body that has been brought under tension.
3. At the end of 5 seconds, breathe out, relax the tense muscles *as much as possible*, focussing your mind on the new relaxed sensations in that part of your body.

4. While letting go (as in (3) above), think of the words 'calm yourself' and 'relax'.
5. Allow your muscles to relax completely and, in your mind, compare the feelings of tension just experienced with the relaxation you now feel.

The particular exercises are as follows:

Arms: Clench the fists and tighten the muscles of both arms, holding your arms stiff and straight out in front of you.

Legs: Raise both legs (or one, if preferred) about 12–18 inches from their resting position, point the toes and stiffen the legs so that thigh and calf muscles are brought under tension. Repeat with other leg if necessary.

General torso: Pull the shoulders back, bringing shoulder blades together, push the chest forward and out and, at the same time, use appropriate muscles to *pull in* the stomach, making a hollow in that part of your body.

Neck: Press the head firmly against the support of the chair back or mattress.

Face: There are three separate exercises here:
(a) Raise the eyebrows, forcing them up as far as you can as if trying to make them meet your hair line.
(b) Screw up your eyes tightly and, at the same time, wrinkle your nose and compress lips hard.
(c) Clench the jaws, as if chewing hard, while pushing you tongue hard against the roof of your mouth.

Remember, each of the above exercises is immediately preceded by taking a deep breath, creating tension, and holding it for five seconds, then exhaling while letting go the tension and saying the work 'relax' to yourself. In each case try to focus your mind on that part of your body that has been made tense and relaxed, in turn.

Don't try to hurry the program of exercises, which should take about 20 minutes or so. After each separate exercise allow a minute or so for fuller relaxation to take place and for you to concentrate on the pleasant sensations that relaxation brings.

Most people need about three weeks of daily training to achieve a useful level of skill, but don't stop at that point. Always keep your practice in relaxation going, although daily training may no longer be required.

It is **very important** that, apart from the training exercises, you should aim to introduce relaxation into your everyday life. For example, keep an eye on the way you brush your teeth, use the vacuum cleaner, or perform any other activity. Does too much muscle tension go into the activity and do you remain in a state of high muscle tension needlessly? Can you sit at your desk, attend a meeting, talk to your wife of husband, help the kids with their homework, or drive your car without considerably more tension than is needed? After performing some quite routine tasks, do you feel a sense of considerable tension and fatigue? Use your relaxation training and the skill developed to counteract these feelings and tendencies.

Some situations, for example in marital conflict, produce very large increases in muscle tension which adds considerably to our feelings of distress. Keeping calm and in control will be a great help in solving these problems and feeling better more quickly and, to meet these specific sources of stress, there is a quick method of relaxation that you can easily acquire. Always try to use the method *before* you lose control, rather than struggling to regain it, having lost out. You may not always get it right, but it is usually possible to anticipate, however briefly, the times of greater stress and to prepare yourself accordingly. Basically, this involves similar procedures as those already described, but the 'exercise' involves whole-body tension and is completed *quickly and unobtrusively in the stress situation*. A little practice will soon create a polished performance. There are two methods, according to the circumstances in which you find yourself.

Method 1

If you are sitting: take a deep breath (quickly and quietly), clasp hands, and press hard against each other, brace leg muscles, pull in stomach muscles, and clench the jaw. Hold for 5 seconds, then exhale, let the tension go and say the word 'relax' to yourself.

Method 2

If you are standing: take a deep breath, clasp hands behind your back, and press hard together, force knees back to create leg muscle tension, pull in stomach muscles, and clench jaws. Hold for 5 seconds, then exhale, let the tension go, and say the word 'relax' to yourself.

Using either method you can quite quickly learn to conceal what it is that you are doing. The tension exerted should not be *wildly exaggerated* but should be certainly felt. Try fixing your eyes on the carpet or on some object near to you while doing the exercise, as if you are really deep in thought for a few moments. To get the full benefit of this quick form of control it is usually helpful to repeat the process two or three times but, altogether, as you will appreciate, this only need take half a minute.

Note If you have any doubt about your physical condition, consult your physician before doing these exercises.